SAUDI ARABIAN STUDENTS IN THE UNITED STATES

Saud Albeshir

Table of Contents

Preface..2

Part I

Chapter One: International students in the United States...12

Chapter Two: Saudi Arabian students in the USA...27

Chapter Three: Education in KSA..41

Chapter Four: Literature on Saudi students in the United States...72

Part II

Chapter Five: The way of life of Saudis in the USA..142

Chapter Six: My story in the United States, the first two years...161

Chapter Seven: My experience in American higher education institutions..192

References...213

Appendix..218

© 2019 By Saud G Albeshir

Preface

Students started traveling overseas to obtain an education nearly 300 years before Christ, beginning with the Greeks traveling to Egypt to advance their understanding of math, science, and art (Good & Teller, 1969). Studying abroad is an old practice that can be noticed in many civilizations during human history. For example, in 607, a Japanese court sent a mission to China to study the empire's education system and one outcome of the visit was the establishment of Japan's first national school system.

Historical references also show that European universities in the Middle Ages were the destination of many foreign students, especially in Italy, France, and Britain. Perraton cited in his book that in England, in 1190, there were two brothers from Friesland (today, the Netherlands) who studied law and rhetoric at Oxford. He also said that around the year 1220, Henry III (1 October 1207 – 16 November 1272), also known as Henry of Winchester, the King of England, gave an open invitation to scholars from the University of Paris who had left the city after a conflict with authorities there. Also, numbers of British traveled to educational institutions abroad, such as Italy, France, and Holland, for educational purposes in the Middle Ages (Perraton, 2014). Over the centuries, the number of foreign students has gradually risen at English universities, and in 2017, 19% of the higher education students in England were foreign students, and 42% of the graduate students were non-European foreign students (The UK Council for International Student Affairs, 2019).

A review of American educational history tells us that rich families living in what is now called the United States send their male children to study at European universities, especially the English universities of Oxford and Cambridge. In 1636, with the opening of the first educational institution in the country, namely Harvard College, a major educational renaissance began in the United States. Nearly a century after the opening of Harvard, the number of institutions of higher education had increased to ten. Notwithstanding the increase in the number of colleges and the educational options in the United States in the eighteenth, nineteenth and twentieth centuries, a large number of Americans preferred to study abroad, especially at European Colleges. Even now, although American universities host the largest number of foreign students in the world, there were 332,727 U.S. citizens studying abroad in 2017, with 54% of these students studying at European universities (Association of International Educators, 2019)

In the Middle East and the Arab countries, where I belong, Egypt was one of the first governments to encourage its citizens to study abroad in European universities in the 19th century. Muhammad Ali Pasha was the ruler [the Khedive] of Egypt from 1805 to 1848, and Ali is considered by many historians the founder of modern Egypt. Ali had wanted to establish a revival and modernization of Egypt. Ali believed that the renaissance in all fields, especially the military and industry, required the presence of educated and skilled hands. Therefore, Ali decided to send a number of Egyptian students to European institutes and universities to learn modern sciences and then transfer the best practices and experiments of these developed countries to Egypt. Egypt officially started its foreign scholarship program in 1813, when a few students were sent to Italy to learn military arts, engineering and other fields of science. Among the Italian cities where the Egyptians studied were Rome, Milan and Florence. A few months later, the Egyptian government sent another 28 students to France and England to learn navigation and mechanics. In 1826, Muhammad Ali ordered about 40 Egyptians to be sent to study overseas in France and major in war sciences; among these 40 students were two sons of Mohammed Ali (Albeshir, 2018).

International students or foreign students can be defined as students who undertake all, or part, of their higher education experience in a country other than their home country, or who travel across a national boundary to a country, other than their home country, to undertake all, or part, of their higher education experience (Institute of International Education [IIE], 2019). The number of international students has risen dramatically over the past few years. According to IIE (2019), the number of foreign international students in higher education in 2001 was 2.1 million, while in 2018, the number of international students was approximately 5 million.

U.S. higher education institutions host the largest number of international students in the world. In 2018, this number was 1.09 million students. Despite the rise in the number of international students in the United States, the USA lost part of its share of the global international student pie. In 2001, the United States colleges accommodated 28% of the total international students, but by 2018, the U.S. hosted 22% of these students, which means that the country lost 6% of its share of the global educational market. Universities in Britain and China were ranked as the second-best educational destinations for studying abroad by 10%, after the United States. Higher education institutions in Australia, Canada, and France have been an educational destination for thousands of foreign students, and each country has attracted 7% of the total international students in the world (IIE, 2019). Chinese students represented the largest percentage of international students in the world in 2016 with almost 32%, followed by Indian students with 16%. Saudi students ranked as the third largest percentage of international students with 5.9%, followed by learners from South Korea, which comprised 5.8% of the total number of global international students. The common academic fields of study that international students participated in in the 2015-2016 academic year were engineering majors (21%), then administration and business (19%).

      The U.S. has dominated the globe in being the most popular university destination for students from all over the world. In the academic year 2017-2018 alone, American institutions hosted 1,094,792 international students, and these non-national students represented 5.2% of the total number of learners in American higher education schools. Many motivations make post-secondary education institutions in the United States attractive to international students, such as the USA having a significant number of the best universities in the world. The USA has always had the top place in the university rankings across the globe; as a result, students in American colleges are more likely to have quality education. In addition to obtaining degrees from the United States giving international students a social status and prestige after returning home, especially graduates from elite universities such as Harvard, Princeton, Columbia, and Yale, another reason international students also aim to study at American universities is for permanent residence, to live and work in the land of liberty. The largest groups of international students in post-secondary education in the United States in 2018 were from

China, followed by Indian students and then South Koreans. The fourth largest group was Saudi international students, and this is the target group of this book.

Higher education institutions in the United States are the preferred educational destination for Saudi students studying abroad. The number of Saudis in the U.S. post-secondary education in 2018 was 44,432 students compared with 5,448 students in 2005. The main reason for the tremendous increase in the number of Saudi students in the United States in recent years is the launch of a government program offering an external scholarship to encourage Saudis to study at the best international universities. This program is called the King Abdullah Scholarship Program. Saudi students who gain the government scholarship receive many advantages while studying abroad: the Saudi government pays the full tuition fees in addition to a monthly salary for each student and other services, such as medical insurance.

About the author

I was born in Riyadh, the capital of Saudi Arabia, at the end of 1987. My parents were well-educated, and both worked as teachers for many years before they retired. They both received master's degrees in education from the United States in the 1980s. I studied K-12 in public schools. In 2006, I graduated from high school with a high GPA, which allowed me to get accepted readily into a public university. I enrolled at King Saud University (KSU) and specialized in deaf education. In 2009, I graduated from KSU with honors. Immediately after graduation, I began working as a teacher for the deaf and hard of hearing at a primary school near the city of Hafr al-Batin. In 2011, I changed employment from a classroom teacher to a teaching assistant at the College of

Education of KSU, my alma mater. At the end of 2011, I was fortunate to earn a government scholarship to take up language and postgraduate studies in the United States. I studied English from 2012 to 2013 in the cities of Pullman and Seattle in Washington. In 2015, I finished my master's in educational leadership from Cleveland State University. In 2016, I started my doctoral studies at Seattle University; however, I did not continue there because the doctorate program was not fit for my scholarship. Therefore, I had to change my university. Also, I was fortunate to choose Indiana State University to study my Ph.D. In 2019, I completed my doctoral program in Educational Administration.

My intention in writing this book was to enrich the content of Saudi students in the United States because the publications are very few. Therefore, I wanted to reduce the gap in the literature of Saudi students in the states by writing this book, which is considered the first book that concentrates on Saudi college students in dreamland. Further, I am interested in writing books in Arabic and English about schools and education in both KSA and the United States. I have written five books; one of them in was in English, which was titled as **Introduction to Public Education in Saudi Arabia**. The other four books were in Arabic and focuses on education in America, including K-12 and higher education. The titles of my books are:

- History of American Education from 1600 to 1913
- American Educational System
- Laws and Trials that Changed the Reality of American Education
- Contemporary Issues in American Education.

The Book's Outline

This book is divided into two main parts; the first part contains four chapters, which are foreign students in the United States, Saudi students in American universities, education in Saudi Arabia, and studies on Saudis in the United States. The second part of the book includes three additional chapters all based on my experiences where I spent a good time in the United States from the end of 2011 to mid-2019 to study in three states, namely Washington, Ohio, and Indiana. The first chapter in the second part presents general topics on the way of living of Saudi students in the United States. The second chapter in part two presents my story in the United States in the first two years I studied English. In the last chapter of the book, I briefly wrote about influential topics in my academic studies when I was a graduate student at three universities in the States.

The first chapter of this book presents valuable information about foreign students in post-secondary educational institutions in the United States. This chapter also contains recent statistics on US universities, including student numbers, funding, and teaching staff. The second part of this chapter provides information on foreign students in the states regarding the most prominent universities that have attracted these non-local student groups, majors, and the economic impact of these foreign learners on the country. The first chapter also discusses the obstacles and difficulties faced by international students in American university studies, according to recent research published in scientific journals.

Chapter two enriches readers about Saudi students at higher education institutions in the United States. The first part of the section provides brief information about the Kingdom of Saudi Arabia, including topics related to culture, politics, and economics. This chapter also aims to highlight the history of Saudi students in the United States, drawing on the few resources available. Further, chapter two recalls the events of September 2001, which negatively affected Arab and Muslim students, especially the Saudis. The second part of this chapter provides details about King Abdullah's external scholarship program, and this government program has been the main reason for the unprecedented increase in the number of Saudi students in the United States in recent years. This chapter also introduces the latest statistics on Saudi students in American educational institutions, including their numbers, majors, and levels of education.

Chapter three briefly presents the most important topics related to education in Saudi Arabia, including public education and higher education. The chapter begins by mentioning remarkable historic events that played a vital role in the beginning stages of public education, including the education of women, which was a hot topic in society a long time ago. The chapter also presents several topics such as the role of the government in education, religion and education, the educational system in the schools, the administrative organization in education, the role of the Ministry of Education, and school funding. The chapter goes on to offer knowledge about the curricula of public schools in Saudi Arabia. The last part of this chapter deals with higher education in Saudi Arabia, which has shown an increase in the number of universities in the past few years. This section also displays statistical data on universities among KSA and Saudis who study aboard.

The fourth chapter shows studies on Saudi international students in the United States. This chapter attempts to present the largest portion of old and new studies on Saudi students in American higher education institutions. It is worth knowing the number of studies on Saudis in the States is limited, and most of these studies are doctorate dissertations. Chapter four is generally divided into two parts, the old and new studies on Saudi students in the United States. The events of September 11, 2001 changed many circumstances and factors that may have had an impact on the results of the studies on Saudis. As a result, I believe it is wise to divide the studies into two parts. The first part shows the studies before the terrorist attack, and the second review studies after the events of 9/11. Further, the second part deals with 13 recent studies in detail published in the last ten years.

The fifth chapter includes various topics linked to the ways of life of students from Saudi Arabia who study at language institutions (ESL) and colleges of the United States. My aim in this section is to pick several significant topics about the Saudis in the United States. Some of the issues may seem a bit unfamiliar, but these topics are essential for documenting a specific and exceptional period that witnessed an incredible increase of Saudis in the States. In this section, I work as much as possible to be objective and convey my perceptions on the lives of Saudi students in the States and my personal experience.

Chapter six briefly presents my story of obtaining a student visa that allowed me to enter the United States as an international student. The chapter also presents exciting details of my experience living in the United States in the first two years and how I tried to develop my English language skills to get accepted to a college. I spent my first two years in the United States in Washington State, and in the first year, I studied English at a language institute in Pullman, which is a city in Whitman County. In the second year, I moved to Seattle to study English at another language institute. Further, the chapter gives details of the cultural differences and challenges I encountered mainly in the first few months as a foreign learner not fluent in English.

Chapter Seven presents some of the challenges and difficulties I encountered during my graduate studies in the United States. The section also shows the most critical differences between the educational environments of Saudi Arabia and America, in my perception. Chapter Seven also highlights some of the issues related to culture, such as students' relationships with their professors and instructors' expectations of their students. At the end of Chapter Seven, which is the last chapter of this book, I address a number of recommendations and advice to people who are in charge of teaching Saudi in both countries to ensure the success of the largest proportion of Saudi students in American universities in the twenty-first century.

Part One

Chapter One: International students in the United States

Chapter One: International students in the United States

In the 1940s, Sen. J. William Fulbright of Arkansas (1905-1995) proposed a government-funded program to promote education and cultural exchange between the United States and other peoples through the spread of tolerance and peace. The proposal was approved and developed into the Fulbright Act (1946), which was named after Sen. J. William Fulbright. This act aims to encourage Americans to study abroad through a government scholarship program that still exists today, and the number of American students who studied abroad was 332,727 in the 2016-17 school year. Fulbright likewise contributed to the increase of foreign students in American higher education institutions. For instance, the number of foreign students in the academic year 1948-49 was 250,460, or 1.1% of the total number of students in American universities, compared with more than 1,094,792 students making up 5.5% of the total enrollment of students in American colleges in the academic year 2017-18 (IIE 2019).

This chapter presents recent data on international students in American higher education institutions. The chapter is divided into three main sections. The first section presents a statistical summary of American post-secondary educational institutions for the academic year 2017-18.The second part of this chapter offers information on international students in the United States, and the last section of this chapter introduces new studies on the obstacles and challenges faced by foreign students studying in the United States.

American Higher education

There are many statistical details available on higher education in the United States and many books' worth of discussion. Consequently, I chose only some primary statistical information that would serve my purpose for this book on higher education in the academic year 2016-17. The main source that I used in this section was the annual report of the National Center for Education Statistics (NCES) called The Condition of Education (2019).

In Fall 2017, a total of 19.8 million students were enrolled in 3,883 degree-granting institutions in the United States. In Fall 2017, total undergraduate enrollment in degree-granting postsecondary institutions was 16.8 million students, an increase of 27 percent from 2000, when enrollment was 13.2 million students. In fall 2017, female students made up 56 percent of total undergraduate enrollment (9.4 million students), and male students made up 44 percent (7.3 million students). In 2017, the majority of students in higher education in America were white, at 8.9 million, followed by Hispanic students, with 3.3 million, then African American students at 2.2 million. Moreover, in 2017, 65% or 10.8 million of all undergraduate students in 2017 studied at 4-year institutions; the remaining 35 percent (5.9 million students) were enrolled in 2-year institutions. Online and distance classes and programs were increasing. In Fall 2017, 5.5 million undergraduate students participated in distance classes, and 2.2 million students, or 13 percent of all undergraduate students, exclusively took distance education courses. Of the 2.0 million bachelor's degrees conferred in academic year 2016–17, more than half were concentrated in five areas of study: business (381,000 degrees), health professions and related majors (238,000 degrees), social sciences and history (159,000 degrees), psychology (117,000 degrees), and biological and biomedical sciences (117,000 degrees;McFarland et al., 2019)

Graduates

Additionally, there was an enormous increase in the number of graduate students in 2017 when compared with 2000. In Fall 2000, there were 2.2 million post baccalaureate students, and in Fall 2017, there were 3 million graduate students for an increase of 39%. In Fall 2017, female students made up 59 percent of total graduate enrollment (1.8 million students), and male students made up 41 percent (1.2 million students). The majority of post-baccalaureate students enrolled in Fall 2017 were white with 1.6 million followed by black with 365,000 students and then Hispanic with 215,000 learners. In Fall 2017, more than one-third of the total graduate students (1.1 million) participated in distance education, with 869,000 students, or 29 percent of total post baccalaureate enrollment, exclusively taking distance education courses. In academic year 2016–17, postsecondary institutions awarded 805,000 master's degrees. Over half of the master's degrees conferred in 2016–17 were concentrated in three fields of study: business, followed by education, the health professions and programs. In 2016–17, the two fields in which the most doctoral degrees were conferred were health professions and related programs and legal professions and studies. (McFarland, et al., 2019)

Faculty

According to NCES (2019), in Fall 2017, there were 1.5 million faculty in degree-granting postsecondary institutions, compared with a million faculty members in 1999, which means the number of faculty members rose

49% from 1999 to 2019. Faculty include professors, associate professors, assistant professors, instructors, lecturers, assisting professors, adjunct professors, and interim professors. In 2017, 53% of faculty were full time, and 47% of them were part-time. Furthermore, between 1999 and 2017, the percentage of faculty who were female increased from 41% to 50%. The majority (76%) of faculty members in 2017 were white (41% and 35% female). (McFarland, et al., 2019)

Funding

The main sources of funds for degree-granting institutions in 2016–17 were tuition and fees; investments; and government grants, contracts, and appropriations. The average of undergraduate tuition and fees for full-time students in 4-year institutions increased by 13 percent between academic years 2010–11 and 2017–18 at both public institutions (from $8,000 to $9,000) and private nonprofit institutions (from $29,800 to $33,800). In contrast, the average tuition and fees at private for-profit 4-year institutions were 5 percent lower in 2017–18 ($14,700) than in 2010–11 ($15,400). A large percentage of Americans depend on loans to fund their college studies. Student loans can come from the federal government or private sources such as banks. However, student loan debt in the US has snowballed into a significant economic crisis, and the total estimated US student loan debt exceeded $1.5 trillion in 2019.

International Students

The total number of students in higher education institutions in the United States for the academic year 2017–18 was 19.9 million, and the number of female students was 11.2 million, which means the majority of students in higher education in the States are females. The number of foreign students in US universities has slightly risen in recent years by 1.5%, and the number of foreign students for the academic year 2017–2018 was 1,094,792 students. Also, during the same academic year, the proportion of foreign students out of the total number of students in higher education in the United States was approximately 5.5%.

Foreign students in higher education institutions study all 50 US states but in unequal proportions. Colleges in California attract more foreign students, with 14.5% of foreign students studying in the Golden State. The second largest proportion of foreign students is in New York with 11% followed by Texas, where 7% of international students learned. Massachusetts, Illinois, and Pennsylvania were also major states to host international students in the academic year 2016–17.

Why do international students come to the U.S. to study?

Multiple reasons encourage international students to go to the United States for post-secondary study:

- Educational quality and academic excellence.
- Americans are friendly with and tolerant of foreigners.
- University campuses in the United States are distinguished by diversity and multiculturalism.
- The opportunities for research, training, and teaching.
- Technological and scientific progress.

- Graduates from American institutes gain social status and prestige in some countries.

Economic Impact of International Students

Foreign students are actively contributing to the growth of higher education economies in particular, which is positively reflected in the US economy in general. For instance, in 2017, foreign students alone contributed $42.4 billion to the US economy and creating 455,000 direct and indirect job opportunities. These billions come from the high tuition fees paid by foreign students; foreign students often pay twice as much tuition fees as local students. This expense is in addition to the personal expenses of these foreign students and their housing and other necessities of daily life. Most (56%) foreign students receive financial support from their families to pursue higher education in the United States. 5.2% of the foreign students have study scholarships from foreign governments or universities such as Saudi students, most of whom rely on funding from the Saudi government (IIE,2019).

International Students by Field of Study (2017-18)

1. Engineering: 21.3%
2. Math and Computer Science: 17.0%
3. Other STEM: 11.5%
4. Business and Management: 17.9%
5. Social Sciences: 7.6%
6. Fine and Applied Art: 5.8%
7. Undeclared and Other: 16.5%
8. Intensive English: 2.4 %. (Open doors, 2018)

Leading Host Universities

According to the open door, (2018) approximately 25% of international students study in 25 universities, with New York University the top university that hosts international students in the US. and the total number of international students in the academic year 2017-18 was 17,552, followed by the University of Southern California ,which hosted 16,075 non-local students. Northeastern University in Boston was ranked the third-biggest educational institution for hosting international students, with 14905 students coming from overseas. Also, Columbia, Arizona State, Illinois, California, and Purdue were among the top universities that attracted outsider students.

Largest Group of International Students in the US

Chinese students were the largest group of foreign students in the United States in 2017-18 and represented 33.2% of the total number of non-local students with 363,341 learners. The second largest group of foreign students for the academic year 2017-18 were from India, and the number of Indian students was 196,271 or 17.9% of the total number of foreign students. Students from South Korea placed the third largest group of foreign students in higher education in the United States with 54,555 students followed by students from Saudi Arabia, which numbered 44,432 students. Canadian students were the fifth largest group of foreign students in the United States followed by students from Vietnam, Taiwan, and Japan.

The Obstacles Encountered by International Students

The complete number of international students in American post-secondary school in the 2017-2018 academic year was 1.09 million (IIE, 2019). However, non-local students encounter some hurdles during their educational journeys in the United States. The principal difficulties for international students are culture, social, financial, and academic (Bai, 2016;Banjong, 2015; Gautam et al., 2016; Gebhard,2012; Hofstede, Hofstede, & Minkov, 2010; Lin & Scherz, 2014; Liu, 2016; Perry, 2016; Trice, 2007;Smith & Khawaja, 2011).

Culture Shock

Culture shock is a primary challenge for international students, particularly in the first periods of arriving in the United States (Geary, 2016; Liu, 2016; Matusitz, 2015; Wu et al., 2015). Young (2014) explained the concept of culture shock as "the emotions and subsequent behaviors brought on by immersion in a new or different cultural situation than that to which one is accustomed" (p. 59). Macionis and Gerber (2010) explained culture shock as "the personal disorientation a person may feel when experiencing an unfamiliar way of life due to immigration or a visit to a new country, a move between social environments, or simply when traveling to another type of life" (p. 54). Also, culture shock explains the impact of moving from a familiar culture to one that is unfamiliar. It includes the shock of a new environment, meeting lots of new people, and learning the ways of a new country. It also includes the shock of being separated from the important people in your life, such as family, friends, colleagues, and teachers: people you can talk to during times of uncertainty; people who offer you support and guidance (UW, 2019). Culture shock generally moves through four phases: honeymoon, frustration, adjustment, and acceptance. International students experience culture shock through differences in language, values, food, and lifestyles (Hofstede et al., 2010; Young, 2014). Language differences are a common problem during international students' adaption and adjustment to U.S. culture (Banjong, 2015; Liu, 2016). One of the cultural challenges for foreign students is making friends with Americans (Perry, 2016; Trice, 2007). Moreover, different traditions and customs are a cultural problem for some international students (Wu et al., 2015). Some international students avoid visiting public sites in their study towns because they do not know the appropriate forms of behavior (Gautam et al., 2016; Kusek, 2015; Wu et al., 2015). A number of international students have also reported that they experience less social interaction and engagement in the local communities while studying in the United States than in their home countries (Kusek, 2015).

Social Issues

International students commonly encounter some social difficulties and problems in American culture (Bai, 2016; Gautam et al., 2016; Matusitz, 2015). Several international students reported feeling lonely while staying in America because they failed to make friends with their American classmates (Banjong, 2015). Lin and Scherz (2014) pointed out also that some international students play a passive role and feel isolated in classrooms. Banjong (2015) also discussed homesickness and loneliness as a hurdle for many international students in America. Moreover, homesickness and loneliness influence international students' performance negatively (Banjong, 2015). Researchers explained that the shortage of language skills is the main source for the social difficulties of foreign students in America (Banjong, 2015; Lin & Scherz, 2014; Wu et al., 2015). Lin and Scherz (2014) and Liu (2016) argued that language differences cause many foreign students to live in isolation because they are uncomfortable speaking English in front of their American classmates. As a consequence, international students do not give their views and thoughts in classes. Moreover, Trice (2007) pointed out that limited English abilities are a reason for international students being isolated from the local community, especially their classmates and instructors. According to Wu et al. (2015), the particularities of speech, such as pronunciation, accent, and speed, isolate many international students. Banjong (2015) argued that inadequate English skills were responsible for international students having a difficult time making friends with Americans. Kusek (2015) studied relationships between international students attending public universities in Ohio and the local communities in a number of small cities. Kusek reported that despite the huge number of foreign students in Ohio, relations with the local community were very poor, and the students had a low level of engagement. Kusek also mentioned that international students had a secure attachment to their study campuses and inadequate social activities compared to when they were living in their home nations. Meanwhile, Kutintara and Min (2016) stated that international students spent less time engaging with sports teams compared to when they were in their homelands.

Financial Problems

A part of the international student community encounters a financial crisis primarily because these students pay higher tuition than domestic students do. International students pay tuition and fees at a rate double or triple that of the local students at US public universities (IIE, 2019). A majority of international students receive financial assistance from their families. The monetary assistance causes additional stress due to the financial burden, and it is attributed to unsatisfactory academic performance (Wu et al., 2015).

Academic Challenges

The language is the primary academic barrier for the majority of international students (Bai, 2016; Banjong, 2015; Constantine, Okazaki, & Utsey, 2004; Gautam et al., 2016; Liu, 2016; Rabia, & Hazza, 2017). Liu (2016) observed a large group of international students had limited English abilities and skills. A large portion of participants suffered from a long list of reading materials compared to that of their home countries. Moreover, some of the sample participants had difficulty understanding their professors' speech, and it was hard for these students to comprehend some of the ideas and idioms of their professors and classmates. According to Liu, Asian international students in America were affected negatively by language in the learning setting. Students had to understand lessons and ask questions to meet their academic requirements. Also, some students reported their professors were not satisfied with their international writing skills, which elevated the writing expectations for students in the college stage (Liu, 2016). Banjong (2015) argued that English skills are the central problem for international students because English is the essence of comprehension in lectures and taking tests in higher education institutions. Further, Rabia & Hazza (2017) concluded that the language barrier was the most obvious challenge among Arab international students in American post-secondary institutions. Rabia & Hazza included problems with the English language as one of the causes of their Arabic participants' difficulties with writing and communication.

Language and Achievement

Several researchers have found significant correlations between the English language proficiency of international students in American higher education centers and academic achievement (Daller & Phelan, 2013; Koys, 2010; Morris & Maxey, 2014; Wait & Gressel, 2009; Ward, Jacobs, & Thompson, 2015). All of these researchers measured English proficiency using Test of English as a Foreign Language (TOEFL) test results. The first measure of academic achievement was Grade Point Average (GPA). According to Ward et al. (2015), the average GPA of international students during their first year at Origin University is lower than that of resident students at the same level due to language challenges. TOEFL test results are a valid indicator for predicting academic success (Morris & Maxey, 2014). Wait & Gressel (2009) noticed that there is a positive and significant connection between TOEFL test results and performance in both comprehensive assessment examination and classrooms among international students who study engineering performance.

Nevertheless, other research claims that international students' TOEFL test results bear no relationship to their academic performance (Krausz, Schiff, Schiff, & Hise, 2005; Martirosyan, Eunjin Hwang, & Wanjohi, 2015; Wongtrirat, 2010). Wongtrirat's (2010) research presents a summary of "the results of a meta-analysis of 22 studies on the connection between English language ability and the academic achievements of international students" (p. 75). The studies that were reviewed had been conducted between 1987 and 2009 using GPA and course completion in conjunction with TOEFL test results for English proficiency to measure academic performance. Wongtrirat concluded that TOEFL test results are not an effective method of predicting the academic achievement of international students. Moreover, Krausz et al. (2005) found that TOEFL test results are not connected with the academic outcome grades of international students in a business college.

summary

This chapter presented an overview of international students in American post-secondary institutions. The number and percentage of non-national students in the United States have grown over time, reaching more than 1.09 million students, making up 5.5% of the total in U.S. colleges in 2017-18. International students receive many advantages from studying in the United States; at the same time, these learners contribute to the growth of the national economy of America. The last section of this chapter discussed the obstacles that meet international students while studying in higher education schools. International students in the US. are more likely to encounter cultural, financial, social, and language barriers as the scholarly literature on international students pointed out. The next chapter deals with Saudi foreign students in higher education institutions in the United States.

Chapter Two: Saudi Arabian students in the US

Chapter Two: Saudi Arabian students in the USA

Arab-American relations are old and date back to the American Revolutionary War (1775-1783). The Arabic country of Morocco was the first country to recognize the United States of America in 1777, but official recognition from Morocco came in 1786 when the leaders of the two countries signed a treaty of peace and friendship (Office of the Historian). Before that, we cannot ignore the role that Arabian horses from Algeria played in the discovery of regions in America during the fifteen century. Later, these types of horses were used by the Founding Fathers to win the independence of the United States from Great Britain in 1776.

After he succeeded in unifying his country on 28 September 1932, King Abdulaziz sought to obtain international recognition for his country. The Soviet Union was the first non-Arab country to recognize Saudi Arabia as an independent state. King Abdul Aziz also aspired to earn the United States' recognition of his country. At the time, the Americans were not interested in Saudi Arabia. In the beginning, King Abdul Aziz's efforts were rejected by Washington, but they eventually changed their position after Saudi Arabia won the recognition of many other countries. The United States formally recognized Saudi Arabia in May 1931 by providing diplomatic recognition. At the same time, King Abdul Aziz signed a concession agreement under which Standard Oil of California was granted the right to prospect for oil in the eastern parts of the country. In return, the company gave the Saudi government $53,000 and paid rent and royalty payments.

The United States, first through its oil industry and then through government contracts, established a relationship with Saudi Arabia's founder, King Abdulaziz Ibn Saud, and his successors, which evolved into a close alliance despite a stark clash in values. U.S. businesses have been involved in Saudi Arabia's oil industry since 1933 when the Standard Oil Company of California (now Chevron) won a sixty-year concession to explore eastern Saudi Arabia. It made its first oil discovery there in 1938 (The Council on Foreign Relations [CFR]).

Saudi-US relations developed very rapidly after the discovery of oil in Saudi Arabia, and Saudi-US interests became linked in political and economic fields. Furthermore, there were interests between Saudi Arabia and the United States in the fifties of the last century and the fight against communism, which spread much of the Arab countries, particularly after the Mohammed Najib then Gamal Abdel Nasser led a military coup in 1952 against King Farouk for control of Egypt, calling for an end of the monarchy and forcing the King and his family to leave Egypt from the port of Alexandria to Europe, where he died in Italy in 1965.

Saudi-US relations have gone through many stages of success and friendship. Saudi Arabia is the loyal partner of the United States in the Middle East. The past decades have witnessed treaties, agreements, and cooperation between the two countries in various fields, especially the military field, where Saudi Arabia buys most of its arms from the United States. The United States also contributed to the liberation of Kuwait in 1991 from the invasion of Saddam Hussein's forces and protected Saudi Arabia from attacks by Iraqi forces at the time. However, Saudi-US relations have been affected by two major incidents. The first was in 1973 when Saudi Arabia and some Arab countries cut the oil off US markets because of the US government's defiance of Israel during the Arab-Israeli war. The second is the events of September 9, 2001, when some of the perpetrators of the terrorist attack were Saudi nationals. The strong relations between the two countries overcame two incidents in a short period; today, Saudi-US relations at their best, and we see many American investors enthusiastic about entering and investing in Saudi Arabia

The chapter aims to find out more about Saudi international students in post-secondary institutions in the United States. The first part of this chapter briefly presents key information about Saudi Arabia, including its cultural and economic aspects. The second part of the chapter presents the history of Saudi students at US colleges. This section recalls the terrorist events of September 2001, which negatively affected Saudi students. The current chapter also contains information on King Abdullah's external scholarship program, which has contributed to the rise in the number of Saudi students in American universities. The last part of the chapter presents data on Saudi students in the United States, including their academic majors and the economic impact of these students on the US economy.

Overview of the Kingdom of Saudi Arabia

KSA is the biggest country in the Arabian Peninsula (Ministry of Foreign Affairs [MFA], 2016). KSA is divided into 13 regions, and each region has its capital. Riyadh is the capital and the biggest city in KSA. Located in the southwest part of Asia, KSA is at the crossroads of Europe, Asia, and Africa. KSA is surrounded by eight countries, which are Jordan, Qatar, Iraq, Kuwait, the United Arab Emirates, the Sultanate of Oman, Yemen, and Bahrain (MFA, 2016).

Population and Economy

According to the General Authority for Statistics (GAS, 2019), KSA population has increased rapidly from 7,000,000 in 1974 to 33,413,660 in 2019. KSA has one of the biggest economies in the world. The oil industry makes up 75% of the budget revenue. Therefore, the oil decline affected the economy significantly. The per capita average was $39,716 in 2015 (GAS, 2016).

Language

The official language in KSA is Arabic (Ministry of Information and Culture [MIC], 2019). Arabic is one of the oldest languages on the earth. Millions of people speak Arabic. Arabic is important for all Muslims because it is the language of the holy book of Islam, the Quran (MIC, 2016). According to United Nations (UN, 2016), 422 million people speak Arabic. Unlike in English, people write and read in Arabic from right to left. Saudi public schools teach all subjects in Arabic, except English lessons.

The Collective Society of Saudi Arabia

The culture of KSA is attempting to create a balance between traditional conservatism and modernism (Abdel–Razek, 2012; Hofstede, 2011; Long & Maisel, 2010). One approach to classifying a culture or society as collective or individualist is by considering the degree of clinging to traditional customs and social values. Societies that demonstrate a high level of these elements are considered collectivistic. In collectivistic societies, group interests are more important than individuals' benefit. In collectivist cultures, individuals value their in-group as a whole, taking into account how their actions have positive or negative consequences on outgroups while staying closely knit with their ingroup (Hofstede, 2011). The KSA culture presents a high degree of collectivism in the world (Abdel–Razek, 2012; Hofstede,2011). In general, in collectivistic societies, the older generations usually represent the wisdom given by experience and to whom others need to listen and learn from. In collectivist cultures, younger people show more respect to seniors (Abdel–Razek, 2012).

Official Religion

Islam is the official religion in KSA, and all Saudis are Muslims (MIC, 2016). Long and Maisel (2010) concluded that the teachings of Islam are the primary influence in Saudi culture, traditions, and education. Therefore, researchers who have an interest in studying the culture of KSA need to have a basic understanding of Islam. Islam is the second largest faith after Christianity, with more than one billion adherents around the world. The word Islam is an Arabic term that means submission to God and peace. Some people think that Islam inspires violence against non-Muslims, but the real Islam is a religion of peace, tolerance, and forgiveness (Council on American-Islamic Relations [CAIR], 2016).

Muslims believe in all prophets of God, such as Abraham, Moses, Jesus, and Muhammad (CAIR, 2016). The Quran is the primary reference of the Islamic religion, and the Quran is the literal word of God as revealed to the Prophet Muhammad, peace be upon him. The Prophet Muhammad lived from 570 AD to 632 AD in the northwest of the Arabian Peninsula (Long & Maisel, 2010).

Political System

In September 1932, King Abdel–Aziz bin Saud united enormous regions of the Arabian Peninsula under the name of KSA (Long & Maisel, 2010). King Abdel–Aziz was the first king of Saudi Arabia and chose the city of Riyadh to be the capital of this country. The political system in Saudi Arabia confirms that the king is the absolute ruler and prime minister (MIC, 2016). The political system in Saudi Arabia indicates that the kingdom is an absolute monarchy, and Islamic law or Sharia is the legal system of the country. The Saudi people cannot participate politically by voting, and opening political parties is illegal (Long & Maisel, 2010).

King Abdel–Aziz died in 1953, and six of his sons became kings of Saudi Arabia from that time until present (MIC, 2016). The first king after King Abdel–Aziz was his son Saud, then King Faisal; the third king was Khaled, followed by King Fahad. The fifth King was Abdallah, who passed away in January 2015. The current king of the country is Salman, and the crown prince is Mohammed bin Salman, who is a second crown prince of the grandson generation of the founder of the country, King Abdel–Aziz (MIC, 2019).

History of Saudi Students in the United State

The government of Saudi Arabia launched a study abroad scholarship program in 1927 by sending 14 Saudi citizens to study in Egypt. KSA did not have higher education institutions at that point. In 1935, the 14 Saudi citizens successfully graduated from Egyptian universities. This inspired and encouraged the Saudi government to expand the study abroad scholarship program. In the 1930s and 1940s, the Saudi government provided financial support to hundreds of citizens so that they could study at Arabic universities, particularly in Egypt and Lebanon. These two countries were among the best-developed Arab countries that had effective educational systems during that time.

Historians differ on when Saudi scholars began to go to Europe, but the largest number of historians has confirmed that 1936 was the year when Saudi students started receiving scholarships to study at European universities. There is also no official information on the start of Saudi scholarships to American universities. However, reports from the Saudi Press Agency indicate that, in 1952, nine Saudis graduated from U.S. universities; perhaps they were the first Saudis to graduate from American universities. Six of the Saudis received master's degrees.

The first Saudi student sent to the United States for higher education

According to a report by the Saudi Cultural Mission in the United States (SACM), the late Abdullah ibn Hamoud Al-Tariki was the first official Saudi scholarship student. Al-Tariki studied for a master's degree in geology at the University of Texas in Austin in 1947 and had obtained a bachelor's degree from an Egyptian university before that. After returning from the US, Mr. Al-Tariki was the first minister of petroleum and mineral wealth in the KSA, and he was a co-founder of the Organization of Petroleum Exporting Countries (OPEC) with the Venezuelan minister in 1960.

With the increase in the number of Saudi students in America colleges, the first non-official cultural office was opened in 1951 to supervise Saudi scholarship students in America, and the office was initially opened as an extension office at the KSA Mission to the United Nations in New York City. In 1956, the Cultural Office was officially opened and independent of the Saudi Office at the United Nations. The headquarters of the Cultural office was in New York. The role of the Saudi Cultural Office was the financial and social supervision of this very small number of Saudis students.

By 1974, the number of Saudi students in the US. colleges were 2039. The main reason for the increase in the number of students was that the Saudi government encouraged its citizens to study at American universities by creating scholarship programs. The Government Scholarship Program aims to provide services to facilitate the work of Saudi students by paying all of their tuition fees, providing health insurance, and paying a monthly government salary.In 1975, the Saudi Cultural Office moved from New York City to Houston, Texas. In 1978, a second Saudi Cultural Office was opened in Los Angeles due to the large number of Saudi students in the western parts of the United States. Later, eight branches of the Saudi Cultural Office were opened throughout the USA.

The number of Saudis in American higher education institutions reached a peak in 1979. Of the 11,000 Saudi students who registered at the Houston office, one-third were females. It is important to note that the statistics on Saudi students during the previous decades are not as accurate as expected, but at present, statistics are more reliable because data is stored on computers. Sadly, after reaching a peak in 1979, the number of Saudi students dropped significantly because of the social revolution in Saudi Arabia during that era, which occurred due to two major events that took place: the Iranian revolution and the siege of the Holy Mosque by a terrorist group.

The World Events

The event of 9/11 was an important factor that influenced the Saudi students in the United States (Heyn, 2013; Shaw, 2010). On September 11, 2001, 19 terrorists related to "Al-Qaeda hijacked four commercial airplanes and purposely crashed two of them into the Twin Towers of the World Trade Center in New York City and one into the Pentagon building in Washington, D.C" (Long & Maisel, 2010, p. 151). The event was the first attack on American soil since the Japanese attacked Pearl Harbor in 1941. Fifteen of the 19 hijackers were Saudis, which led to the lack of confidence between the United States and KSA (Long & Maisel, 2010; Shaw, 2010).The event impacted a huge number of countries and people. After the event, President George W. Bush declared war on terrorists and Al-Qaeda followers (Cainkar, 2009). Muslims and Arabs inside the United States became victims of Al-Qaeda's attack. According to Cainkar (2009), the attacks and hate crimes against Muslims increased rapidly after 9/11. Many individuals thought Arabs and Muslims were not loyal to the country. The U.S. officials also deported many illegal immigrants from Arabic countries following the 9/11 attack. International students, especially Muslims and Arabs, were victims of the world event as well (Urias & Yeakey, 2005). Some of the 19 terrorists who attacked on 9/11 held a student visa to enter the country. Therefore, the conventional forces interviewed more than 1,000 Arab and Muslim students about the relationship between these students and the terrorist attacks. The officials added more regulations and processes needed to receive a student visa after the attacks (Urias & Yeakey, 2005).

Saudi students in the United States post 9/11

The events of September 11, 2001 generally had a negative impact on Saudi students in the US. In the first few months after the attack, Saudis found it difficult to obtain US visas of any kind, including for tourism, study, and even commercial purposes. This caused significant problems for the Saudis who had always considered the United States as a favorite tourist and study destination. Fortunately, the political leaders in Saudi Arabia and the United States managed to overcome the effects of the events of September quickly. This is because the United States knows that Saudi Arabia is the most anti-terrorism country and is always looking out for peace and global stability. Starting in 2005, the number of Saudi students in the United States began to increase rapidly due to the launch of a government program for an external scholarship called the King Abdullah External Scholarship Program.

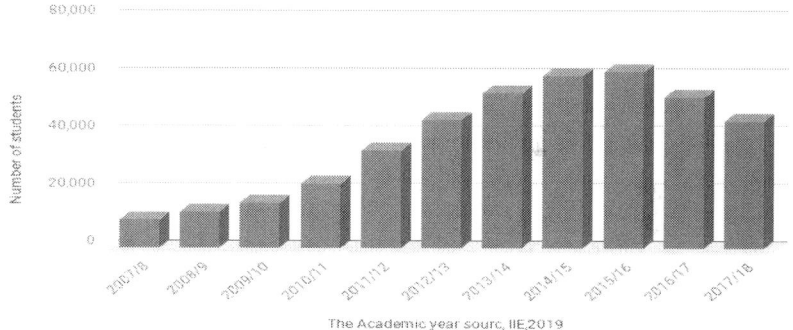

The Academic year sourc, IIE,2019

King Abdullah Scholarship Program

In 2005, the late King Abdullah Bin Abdulaziz Al Saud responded to concerns for the sustainable development of human resources in Saudi Arabia by launching the King Abdullah Scholarship Program (KASP). Supported by the Saudi government and implemented by the Ministry of Education (MOE), KASP would become an important source of support for the kingdom's public and private sectors by developing, qualifying, and preparing human resources. The program would achieve its objectives by sponsoring academically distinguished Saudi citizens to study in the world's best universities, in degree specializations selected in accordance with the needs of the Saudi labor market. Upon completion, graduates would be expected to return to the kingdom and contribute to the country's development (Ministry of Education).

The King Abdullah Scholarship Program for Saudi students in the US

According to SACM (2016), KASP came from the deep belief of the Saudi government that education is a major factor in developing the country. The KASP began in 2005 when the king had an agreement with former American President George W. Bush to increase the number of Saudi students in higher education in the United States. The KASP provides all support for Saudi students to succeed academically.

Students planning to earn a scholarship for King Abdullah's bachelor's degree program must meet the following requirements:

- Cumulative Grade Point Average (GPA) in high school of more than 90 percent.

- The candidate must not exceed 22 years of age.

- The candidate must not be a government employee.

- The candidate agrees to be a full-time student after receiving the scholarship (SACM, 2016).

All students sponsored by KASP receive the following privileges:

- Full academic tuition

- Monthly salary

- Health insurance coverage

- An annual round-trip ticket for the student and his family

- Academic supervision (SACM, 2016)

Overview of Saudi Students in the United States

There is a disparity in the number of Saudis studying in post-secondary education institutions in the United States. According to the Saudi General Authority for Statistics (GAS, 2019), the number of Saudi students registered in the United States was 71,472, of whom 17,773 were female. On the other hand, Open Doors (2019) showed that the total number of Saudi students in the academic year 2017/18 was 44,432 Saudi students in all studies. The number of Saudi students in the United States gradually decreased after reaching a peak in the academic year 2014/15, where the number of Saudis was 59,945 (IIE, 2019).

Fields of study and academic levels

The total number of Saudi international students in 2017/18 was 44,432; the majority of these students were undergraduate students (27,646 or 62%). The graduate students were 11,022 or 24.8%. The most fields of study studied by Saudis in the academic year 2017/18 were engineering (31.4%), followed by business administration (19%), then mathematics and computer science (9.2%). Humanities, social sciences educational disciplines, and fine arts were not very attractive to the Saudis studying in America.

Fields of Study -Saudi international students in The USA 2017-18
Source : IIE,2019

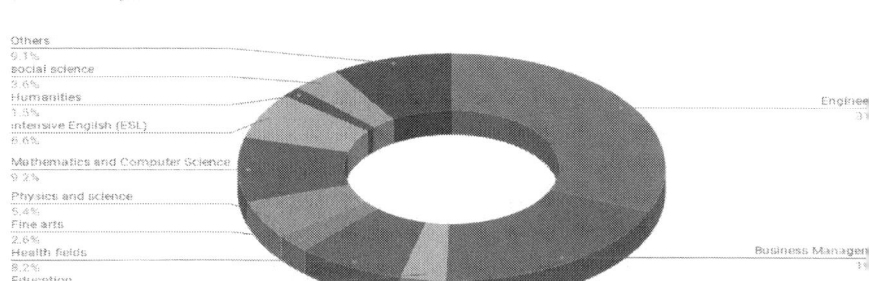

The economic impact of Saudi students

In the academic year 2017/18, the Saudis were the fourth largest group of international students in the United States, following Chinese, Indians, and South Koreans. Saudis as international students typically pay three times more in tuition fees compared to local state students at public universities, and these expenses paid by Saudis are a great economical source for American universities that makes universities welcome international students. Further,

Saudi students and their families have contributed significantly to the growth of the US economy in recent years. In 2017 alone, the Saudis added 1,876 billion dollars into the US economy.

Summary

This chapter presents an overview of Saudi students in higher education institutions in the United States in the past as well as in present times. The chapter reveals that in recent years, there has been a significant increase in the number of Saudi students in the United States due to King Abdullah's external scholarship program, which opened the way for Saudis to come and study in the U.S. In the next chapter, we will learn about schools and education in Saudi Arabia, and the chapter is significant for comprehending the upcoming section of the book that deals with studies related to Saudi students in post-secondary educational institutions in the United States.

Chapter Three: Education in KSA

Education in KSA

Chapter three briefly presents the most important topics related to education in Saudi Arabia, including public education and higher education. The chapter begins by mentioning remarkable historic events that played a vital role in the beginning stages of public education, including the education of women, which was a hot topic in society a long time ago. The chapter also presents several topics such as the role of the government in education, religion and education, the educational system in the schools, the administrative organization in education, the role of the Ministry of Education, and school funding. The chapter goes on to offer knowledge about the curricula of public schools in Saudi Arabia. The last part of this chapter deals with higher education in Saudi Arabia, which has shown an increase in the number of universities in the past few years. This section also displays statistical data on universities among KSA and Saudis who study aboard.

The current Saudi Kingdom was established in 1932, and since that time, the government of the country has had a sincere belief that education is the key to opening future doors. Before creating the Ministry of Education in 1953, there were many attempts by the society and government to educate children and reduce the illiteracy rate, which was very high. Historically, many Arab families sent their boys to learn the basics of religion, reading, and writing in a place called Kuttatebe, but girls at that time were less likely to have the opportunity to get an education. However, there were tens of women who could read and write, mainly in urban areas such as Mecca and Jeddah.

In the Kuttatebe, students learned the traditional forms of knowledge, like memorizing parts of the Holy Quran and understanding Islamic teachings. Teachers were usually religious men who had mastered the essential skills of the time, like reading and writing. Kuttatebe was a private school, so only boys from wealthy or middle-class families could afford the price of a teacher, which was mostly paid in food such as dates or bread.

Readers need to know that the western province, or Hijaz, of the kingdom has a unique history compared to other regions of the country because the two holiest sites for Muslims are there. Hijaz hosts millions of Muslims worldwide every year. Pilgrims from multiple nations and cultures visit Mecca, which is the most sacred site for Muslims and Al-Medina. This is where the prophet Muhammad (peace be upon him) (571- 632) is buried. Hence, Hijaz was well developed compared to other districts of the KSA at that time.

Due to pilgrims, education in Hijaz was affordable in a few places, especially places of worship like mosques. Students studied religious subjects like reading the Holy Quran and listening to stories about the prophet Muhammad (peace be upon him). In 1858, a group of Indian pilgrims established the first modern school in Mecca with full funding coming from an Indian Muslim scholar. The school started inside the Great Mosque of Mecca; later it moved to another building in Mecca. The school was called Al-Soltiah, and it taught Islamic subjects, Arabic, and science. In 1864, an Indian scholar created the second formal school in Mecca and applied the same system of education as in Al-Soltiah. The third formal school in Hijaz opened in Jeddah in 1905. Jeddah is the closest port to Mecca (43 miles) and the port where pilgrims arrive by ship.

King Abdul Aziz believed that education was one of the central foundations for the establishment of a strong nation. The king founded the Directorate of Knowledge in 1923. The first step of formal education started even before some of the regions joined to unite with the founder, King Abdul Aziz, and declared themselves an official country in 1932 under the name the Kingdom of Saudi Arabia. Educators who worked with the Directorate of Knowledge were responsible for the 4 schools in the country. In 1926, the Directorate of Knowledge also built 12 schools in the main cities of the country. By 1952, there were 306 schools in the KSA.

In 1953, the king of the country at that time, Saud, changed the Directorate of Knowledge into the Ministry of Knowledge. The government supported the new ministry with a large budget because the illiteracy rate was high among Saudis. Also, the government wanted to enlighten and modernize the people so they could coexist with the new economy, especially after the discovery of oil in the country. The first minister of knowledge was Prince Fahad before he became the king of the country.

It is important to mention that the Ministry of Education's name has changed three times in almost 65 years. However, the function of the ministry is still the same, which is to promote education, build schools, and reduce illiteracy in society. In 2003, King Fahad, who was the first Minister of Knowledge, ordered the name of the ministry to be changed to the Ministry of Education.

Women's Education in Saudi Arabia

Teaching females in schools was not an easy task for the Saudi government at that time. The families who were fundamentalists believed these schools would corrupt their girls and teach them immorality. These families thought schools would change the values of society and encourage the values of modernity. Historically, fundamentalists in the KSA were against some of the government orders because the government helps modernization in social and economic aspects. For instance, fundamentalists were against opening the first official TV network in 1962, and against sending girls to public schools.

King Faisal and his government encouraged families to send their girls to schools. Also, the government sent many groups of employees who still lived in deserts to the countrysides to explain the importance of girls' education to society. The government explained to the society in schools that girls would learn religion, reading, writing, and how to prepare to be a good mother to the next generation of the nation. However, many families disagreed about sending their girls to schools in the first years of formal education for females. King Faisal, the leader of the country at the time, insisted on teaching women despite the rejection of society. The king did not force families to send their children to public schools. At the same time, he built hundreds of schools for females to make education affordable for those who wanted to learn. It is essential to know that formal education is not compulsory in the KSA but accessible for free in all districts of the country.

The official start of girls' education in the KSA was 1959, when the King ordered the building of schools for girls at all levels of education. In 1960, the government created The General Presidency for Girls' Education to function as the ministry of education for girls. The leaders of The General Presidency for Girls (GPG) worked hard to open schools, and they opened 15 elementary schools for girls in 1960. In the same year, GPG also opened a school to prepare female teachers to teach in girls public schools and accepted 21 students who graduated from private schools. In 1963, the GPG opened in Mecca the first female public school in the country. By 1981, the number of girls and boys in public schools was almost equal, which meant a high success for the government that wanted the best for its citizens and to empower women in the community.

It is important to mention that there were a few private schools for girls before public schooling for girls was established in 1959. For example, Dar-Alhanan in Jeddah was the first modern private school for girls in the KSA, and it was established in 1955. Dar-Alhanan was entirely supported and funded by Queen Iffat, the wife of King Faisal. Furthermore, some rich families sent their children to be educated abroad. Egypt and Lebanon were the top countries that Saudi families chose for their children because they used to have effective educational systems and were developed countries compared to the KSA at that tim. The General Presidency of Girls' Education played a historical role in enlightening hundreds of thousands of Saudi females for 42 years before merging with the Ministry of Education in 2002. Currently, Saudi public schools have more female teachers than male teachers. Further, more Saudi females graduate from universities than males.

The Government and Education

The Saudi government has fully supported education since King Abdulaziz united the country. The government fully funds the Ministry of Education and the building of public schools. Readers need to know that the government does not charge the citizens taxes. The government also supports needy students with a monthly payment so these students will not have to leave school and work to feed themselves. Students with disabilities also receive a monthly salary from the government, along with free transportation and access to help with learning skills such as Braille. Not only does the government support primary education, but it also funded many public universities and colleges that cover all areas of the KSA. In 2015, there were 1,527,769 students in public higher education and all of these students studied for free. At the same time, the government supports all students in higher education with a monthly salary. Moreover, the government is sending thousands of citizens to complete their higher education at top universities around the world. In 2014, almost 115,000 Saudi students studied abroad in 22 countries. The government paid full tuition for these students and also supported them with salaries. It is clear that the government of Saudi Arabia has a deep belief that education is the way to develop the country. Due to this belief, it has spent billions of dollars to invest in the Saudi people.

Special Education

The first official launch of special education services for disabled people in Saudi Arabia was in 1962 when the first public administration for the disabled was established in the ministry of education. Before, in 1962, there was only one official Institute for Blind Students in 1960 in the capital, Riyadh. It is fair to mention that Abdullah Al-Ghanim is considered the godfather of special education in Saudi Arabia, where he participated in the opening of many schools for the blind around the country. Al-Ghanim also supported applying the Arab Braille method, which is an educational aid to help this group of students read by touching symbols in the kingdom. It is interesting to know that Ahmed Al-Bahsin imported the Arab Braille method in 1977 from Iraq to help his blind child learn. Later, Al-Bahsin taught a group of educators to deal with the Arabi Braille alphabet, and one of Al-Bahsin's students was Al-Ghanim, who believed deeply in the abilities of blind students.

After establishing the Department of Special Education in the Ministry of Education, the number of schools and programs that aimed to educate children with all types of disabilities increased sharply. For illustration, in 1964, the Department of Special Education opened the first Institute for Deaf Students in Riyadh with two buildings: one for girls and the other for boys. Deaf students in this institution study subjects through Arabic sign language, which is totally different from American sign language. The last group of disabled students the ministry of education served consisted of learners with autism. In 1996, the ministry opened three programs to help students with autism.

Programs and institutes of students with disabilities started in isolated schools, so these schools have only a group of students, such as only deaf students, in a special school building. Historically, isolated schools were a common way to teach students with disabilities around the world, even in first-world countries like the USA. Happily, in

1996, the leaders of the Ministry of Education started the integration of students with disabilities into normal schools.

According to government data, the disability rate in Saudi Arabia is between 7 and 10 percent of the population of nearly 33 million people. Marriage to relatives may be a cause of high disability in the country because it is very common, so the government encourages pre-marital medical examination to try to reduce genetic disability as far as possible. In 2011, the total number of disabled students in public schools was 39,745 boys and 16,731 girls. These students were divided into eight types of special academic programs, covering the entire territory of the country.

The academic programs that the public schools provide are for students who are hearing impaired, visually impaired, learning disabled, and learners with multiple disabilities. Moreover, the schools serve students who are emotionally unstable, autistic, communicatively impaired, and physically disabled. The ministry also serves minor mentally retarded students academically. There were a total of 3,926 special education programs in 2011. All disabled students in the country receive a monthly salary from the government, free transportation, and free breakfast in their schools. The government also provides all education aids to these students, such as hearing aids for deaf children and braille printers for students with visual issues. Readers need to know that the Ministry of Education gives a financial advantage to teachers who work with disabled children to motivate them.

Illiteracy

The Ministry of Education created a particular administration for adult education and literacy in 1958. It was called the Department of Popular Culture, which was connected to the administration of primary schools in the Ministry of Education. Before that time, the rate of illiteracy was high among the people of the KSA in most regions. Historically, in the first years of formal education in the KSA, many people did not value modern schooling because they needed their children to work with them because of poverty. Also, a significant number of Bedouins were continually moving from one place to another to find sources of water, so their children missed the opportunity for stability and admission to a school.

In 1972, the leader of the country, King Faisal, approved the adult education and literacy system, which encouraged citizens to learn basic educational skills, such as reading and writing. The government also encouraged the people who served in the public sectors, like soldiers and workers, to study. The plan gave them financial advantages after finishing each level of school. The government succeeded spectacularly in reducing illiteracy among Saudis in a short time. In 1972, 60% of people 15 years and over could not read or write, but that dropped to 5.3% in 2012. Also, in 2012, 98.7% of children between 6 and 15 years were school students. The Ministry of Education offered several programs to reduce the illiteracy rate, such as summer camps and classes throughout the year, and the number of academic courses on literacy was 3,706 in 2012 and covered all the territories in the country.

Educational System in Saudi Arabia

The purpose of education

The purpose of Saudi education is to understand Islam correctly; instill and promote the Islamic faith, values, and teachings; provide them with knowledge and skills to develop useful behavioral aims strengthen society economically, socially, and culturally; and prepare individuals to be beneficial members of society.

Ministry of Education Vision and Mission Statements

Vision Statement:

Distinguished learning to build an educated society that can compete globally.

Mission Statement:

Our mission is to provide the opportunity for education for all in an appropriate educational environment in the light of the educational system of the kingdom; to raise the quality of its products, increase the effectiveness of scientific research, encourage creativity and innovation, develop community partnerships, and improve the skills and abilities of education personnel.

The General Foundations of Education in the Kingdom of Saudi Arabia

- The general foundations of education in the Kingdom of Saudi Arabia include a belief in Allah (the God) as Lord, the Islamic religion, and Muhammad (peace be upon him), a prophet of Allah.

- The ideals of Islam for the establishment of human civilization are rational, constructive, and guided by the message of Muhammad (peace be upon him) to achieve a good life in this world and survival in the afterlife.

- We believe in the human dignity that the Holy Quran has decreed and entrusted to the faithful of God on Earth.

- Opportunities are available to students to contribute to the development of the society in which they live. Thus, they will benefit from the development in which they participate.

- The government has to encourage students to learn about their religion at all levels of education.

- Religious sciences are essential in all years of primary, intermediate, and secondary education, and Islamic culture is essential in all years of higher education.

- Students benefit from all kinds of useful human knowledge in the light of Islam, which they can use to raise the nation and its standard of living.

- The use of technology and the sciences is promoted as one of the most important means of cultural, social, economic, and health development to elevate our nation, our country, and our role in global cultural progress.

- Education is linked at all stages of the general development plan of the state.

- There is a conscious interaction with global cultural developments in the fields of science, culture, and literature by following and participating in them and directing them to the benefit of society and to the good and progress of humanity.

- Students learn respect for the public rights that Islam guarantees to preserve security and to achieve the stability of the society.

- Social solidarity is formed among the members of society through cooperation, love, brotherhood, and prioritizing of public interest.

- The character of the Kingdom of Saudi Arabia is distinguished by its protection of the sanctities of Islam; its preservation of the sanctuary of revelation; its adoption of Islam as a doctrine, as worship, as law, and as a constitution of life; and its sense of great responsibility in leading humanity to Islam and guiding it toward the good.

- Arabic is the language of instruction in all subjects and all stages except when it is necessary to teach one in another language.

Religion and Education

Unlike the secular education system in Western countries, the general foundations of education in Saudi Arabia depend on Islamic teachings. Schools teach religion intensively at all levels of education. Students in public schools take an average of 12 classes a week that discuss topics on the religion of Islam. Also, students and teachers do the noon prayer in all public schools every day. Public schools do not teach students philosophy and theories that are contrary to the Islamic religion, such as Darwin's theory of evolution. Moreover, boys and girls study in different school buildings to obey Islamic guidance. Female pupils in middle and high schools are required to wear an Islamic dress that covers their hair when riding on school buses and when they enter and leave school.

Education Funding

In the KSA, the government is fully funding the Ministry of Education to operate public schools and public higher education institutes. The government wholly finances public schools, including all components of schoolhouses, such as facilities, teacher and staff salaries, building operation costs, student books, and monthly payments for students with disabilities. Unlike the governments of most countries, the Saudi government does not tax residents at all, which means that all the costs of public education come from the general state budget. As shown in budget tables, the ministry is spending more money every year due to the enormous increase in the number of public school students. It is important to know that this budget is for primary education (K–12) only, and the money for higher education is not included in the table.

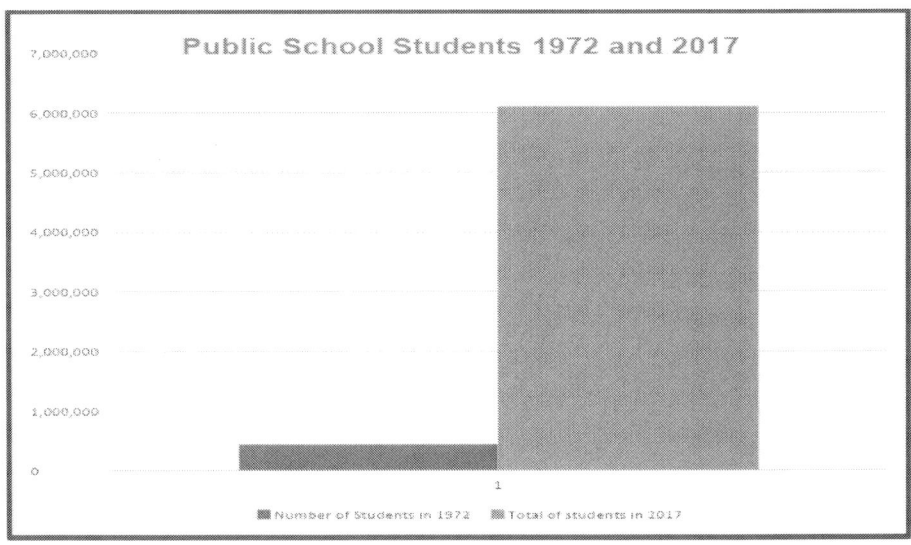

Budget of the Ministry of Education (K-12 only) In Saudi Riyal	
1$ = 3.75 Riyal	
2010	90,000620,000
2011	94.656,037,000
2012	101,466,583,000
2013	118,425,732,000
2014	121,253,000,000
2015	127,442,168,000
2016	124,319,484,000

The Minister of Education

The minister of education is the chief government official on education in the country and is appointed by order of the king. In 2015, the king ordered the integration of the Ministries of Education and the Ministry of Higher Education into a single department called the Ministry of Education. The role of the minister is to make decisions and observe all levels of education, including public and private schools and universities. Ten ministers have led the education of Saudi Arabia. The first minister was Prince Fahd before he became the king of the country. The current minister is Dr. Hamad Al Al-Sheikh.

Educational Levels in Saudi Public Schools

Pre-primary education

Over the last few years, the Ministry of Education has opened tens of pre-primary education schools, but the schools for this stage are still not enough for all children. Accordingly, the number of students in this stage is way lower than those in primary education. In these schools, students from the ages of three to five learn essential skills in life such as using the bathroom by themselves. Also, female teachers prepare young male and female children psychologically, academically, and intellectually to move to elementary school.

Elementary schools

Elementary schools serve students from six years old. Saudi elementary schools have six grades. In 2017, there were 3,166,986 total students in public elementary schools, and 1,559,954 of these students were female. It is essential to remember that there is separation based on gender in schools in the KSA educations except for in preschools. In 2017, there were 6322 public elementary schools for girls and 6339 for boys. The academic year usually starts in September and ends on the first day of May. Elementary students' study two semesters a year, and each semester is 16 weeks. Also, students enjoy two to three short holidays during the academic year. The first day of the school week is Sunday, and students spend five days in school. The students spend their days in school from 7 a.m. to 1 p.m. During this time, they have two breaks. The first one is in the morning to eat their snacks and play with their friends. The second break is for noon prayer. Elementary students have six classes a day, and the length of each course is 45 minutes. At this level, pupils study many subjects, including math, science, religion, and English. The students need to succeed in six academic years to move on to middle school.

Middle Schools

After finishing elementary school, students move to middle school, where they spend three academic years. In 2017, the total number of students in public middle schools was 1,473,413, and the number of males was 752,353. The number of public middle schools has increased sharply in recent years. In 2017, there were 3683 female and 3897 male schools that served all areas of the country.

Middle schoolers study 36 weeks a year, which is divided into two semesters. They commonly begin the academic year in September and end in May. All students in public schools follow the ministry of education, so schools start and finish together around the country. Students at this level of schooling spend five days a week, beginning on Sunday, and enjoy two weekend days, which are Friday and Saturday.

Middle schoolers take more exams than elementary students, and they face more challenging tasks. Students learn many subjects in middle school, such as science, mathematics, religion, history, geography, and linguistics. The school day starts at 7 a.m. and goes until 2 p.m., and students have eight periods of classes; each one is 45 minutes. There are two break times for the students. The first break is in the morning, which is 30 minutes when the students can have some snacks and rest time. The second break is at noon prayer at the end of the school day where students pray together in a prayer room inside the school building.

High schools

Students who finish their middle school years successfully move on to high school in order to spend three more years in school. The total number of high schoolers in 2017 was 1,468,913 students, and 787,468 of the students were boys. In 2017, the number of female public high schools was 2,028 while the number of male schools was 1,966.

The high schoolers start their academic year in September and finish in May. They study two semesters a year, and each semester is 18 weeks long. The students begin their school day at 7 a.m. and leave at 2 p.m. During this time, they take eight classes a day and have two breaks, just like middle schoolers.

The high school stage is critical for students who plan to go into higher education, and learners work hard to make high grades. In the Saudi education system, high school students need to achieve an appropriate level of education in order to be admitted to higher education institutions. Students are measured by their last years' grade point average in high school and by two other tests that are similar to the SAT and ACT in the United States.

All students in their first year of high school study the same subjects, including religion, science, English, and other social sciences. Students in high schools generally have more exams compared to middle school students. In their second year of high school, students need to choose their track, and schools mostly provide two options of major. The first one is the science track, and the second one is religious studies. Students who choose the science track study intensively scientific subjects such as physics, geology, chemistry, biology, and mathematics. On the other hand, students who choose the religious track learn the Arabic language, Islamic faith, and social sciences.

Curricula

The Ministry of Education applies the national curriculum module to all public schools in the country. All students, female and male, in all districts study for free from the exact same textbooks that the ministry publishes. The ministry has experts and scholars that design and write textbooks for students in all fields and grades.

Experts who work on the committee of national curricula try to cover the most important and useful topics in the arts and sciences. For example, students will cover math, science, fine art, and languages. Teachers also receive teachers' books from the committee of national curriculums to help them understand the best way to teach the lessons and identify the lesson goals.

It is important to remember that the foundations of education in Saudi Arabia are Islamic and all schoolbooks follow the philosophy of Islam. Students in all grades study religion intensively while in school. For example, on a daily basis, students learn the Islamic creed and read the holy book of Islam.

Saudi public schools don't teach topics that leaders of the Ministry of Education believe are incompatible with Islam. For example, students have the opportunity to study philosophy because it discusses topics regarding theology and the universe. Also, students do not learn theories at odds with Islamic viewpoints, such as Darwin's theory of evolution.

In recent years, education leaders have introduced ways to modernize the idea of design books and start using technology and social media sites to make learning more accessible to students. Today, the ministry posts all lessons on the national curricula on YouTube, so when a student misses a school day, he or she will have an opportunity to learn online. Also, the ministry is working on a plan to give each student a tablet that has all the books they need to have a good academic performance.

Higher education in Saudi Arabia

The history of higher education in Saudi Arabia is a modern one compared to higher education in the United States, where the first higher education institution, Harvard University, was opened in 1636. The first institution of higher education in Saudi Arabia started in 1951, with the opening of the College of Sharia (Islamic Studies). It is located in the city of Mecca, which is the most sacred city to Muslims. In 1954, the government opened the second higher education institution in Mecca, Teacher College. In 1957, the first university in Saudi Arabia, King Saud University, was opened in the Saudi capital of Riyadh. The government's deep faith in education has pushed it to spend billions annually to expand higher education and make it available to citizens in all Saudi regions, which has led to an increase in the number of higher education institutions. According to the Educational Statistic Center (ESC, 2018), there were 87 higher education institutions in Saudi Arabia in 2018, including 37 public higher education institutions (30 universities and 7 colleges). There were 51 private institutions and 12 private universities in 2018. In the 2014-2015 academic year, 1,311,490 students were enrolled in post-secondary education programs; 1,232,629 were enrolled in public post-secondary programs, and 78,798 at private institutions (ESC, 2016).

Higher Education Students by institution 2016

*The information from Statistical Yearbook of 2018 | Issue Number: 54 by General Authority for Statistics

Educational institution	Total	Graduate	Bachelor
Umm Al-Qura Uni.	107,432	3,174	102,237
Male	50,783	1711	48,293
Female	56,649	1463	53,944
The Islamic Uni.	16,372	3,652	11,703
Male	16,372	3652	11,703
Female	0	0	0
Imam Moh. Ibn saud Islamic Uni.		8,318	107,609
Male		4172	63,068
Female		4146	44,541
King Saud Uni.	62,221	8,151	49,501
Male	37,030	3610	31,182
Female	25,191	4541	18,319
King Abdulaziz Uni.	163,979	6,183	156,505

Female	37,319	1294	35,320
king saud bin Abdulaziz for health Sciences	10,230	1,180	9,050
Male	4,744	656	4,088
Female	5,486	524	4,962
Jazan Uni.	58,466	242	54,306
Male	22,786	108	20,959
Female	35,680	134	33,347
Hail Univers	36,901	504	35,642
Male	12,901	258	12,280
Female	24,000	246	23,362
AL-Jouf Uni.	28,332	78	27,263
Male	12,221	39	11,757
Female	16,111	39	15,506
Tabuk University	34,951	1,079	32,214
Male	14,912	420	13,647
Female	20,039	659	18,567
ALBaha University	23,080	522	22,558
Male	10,439	272	10,167
Female	12,641	250	12,391

Najran University	20,057	301	17,441
Male	8,229	142	7,416
Female	11,828	159	10,025
Princess Noura bint Abdulrahman University	43,038	388	38,578
Male	0	0	0
Female	43,038	388	38,578
University of Northern Border	23,698	56	19,959
Male	12,024	20	10,118
Female	11,674	36	9,841
Shagra University	34,240	0	31,655
Male	14,747	0	13,938
Female	19,493	0	17,717
Prince Sattam Bin Abdulaziz University	30,602	353	28,726
Male	12,594	187	11517
Female	18,008	166	17209
iMam ABDULRAHMAN. Bn FAISAL Uni. 1	81,886	2,042	75,466
Male	22,129	666	21,306
Female	59,757	1376	54,160

Male	86,161	2638	82,639
Female	77,818	3545	73,866
King Fahd Uni. Of Petrol & Min.	12,324	1,629	9,295
Male	12,324	1629	9,295
Female	0	0	0
King Faisal Uni.	165,330	2,839	161,204
Male	102,507	1175	100,961
Female	62,823	1664	60,243
King Khalid Uni.	65,769	2,306	56,466
Male	27,345	1042	23,423
Female	38,424	1264	33,043
Qassim Uni.	72,392	2,428	67,822
Male	28,719	1055	25,550
Female	43,673	1373	42,272
Taibah Uni	64,133	1,983	57,744
Male	25,607	915	23,365
Female	38,526	1068	34,379
Taif Uni.	64,674	2,415	61,138
Male	27,355	1121	25,818

Majmaah University	20,778	312	19,269
Male	11,866	267	10,503
Female	8,912	45	8,766
Saudi Electronic University	19,441	1,148	18,293
Male	12,260	753	11,507
Female	7,181	395	6,786
Jeddah University	14,326	2,173	12,153
Male	8,074	1071	7,003
Female	6,252	1102	5,150
Bisha University	16,982	459	15,491
Male	5,095	158	4,484
Female	11,887	301	11,007
Hafr al batin University	17,591	0	17,407
Male	2,299	0	2,115
Female	15,292	0	15,292
University's Total		53,915	1,316,695
Male		27,737	618,102
Female		26,178	698,593
General Organization for Technical and Vocational Training	133,028	0	4,592

Male	105573	0	4,592
Female	27455	0	0
Prince Sultan Military Fac. for Health Science, Dhahran	997	0	913
Male	596	0	512
Female	401	0	401
AL-Jubail & Yanbu Industrial Faculties	18,271	0	8,567
Male	14,778	0	5,074
Female	3,493	0	3,493
I.P.A	3,996	353	0
Male	3,387	353	0
Female	609	0	0
Private Higher Education	78,614	4,129	74,450
Male	37,407	2340	35,047
Female	41,207	1789	39,403
Total		58,397	1,405,217
Male		30,430	663,327
Female		27,967	741,890

Funding

Unlike many countries, higher education in Saudi Arabia is free in public universities and is funded entirely by the Saudi government, which means that students in public universities study without tuition fees. In addition, the Saudi government encourages citizens to continue higher education and provides them with a monthly salary for every student in public universities, about $200 per month. Also, the government provides low-cost meals for students and free accommodation for foreign students who do not have housing.

Government Expenditure on education

Government Appropriations for Education, by Institute (In millions of SR) from General Authority for statistics in KSA

- **One million Dollar is worth 3.75 million Saudi Riyals**
- ***The Saudi government spent more than $ 57 billion on education in 2015**

Institutes	2014-2015	2013-14	2012-13
Institute Of Public Administration	443	437	412
King Abdul Aziz's Darat	43	42	40
Ministry of Education	117,666	113,180	110,326
Higher Education	21,128	21,168	21,157
King Saud University (Riyadh)	6,619	6,685	6,570

King Abdul-Aziz University Jeddah	4,372	4,391	4,144
King Fahad University for Petroleum & Minerals	945	974	961
Imam Mohammad Bin Saud Islamic University	2,915	2,881	2,569
King Faisal University	1,112	1,096	1,004
Umm Al-Qura University	2,136	2,079	1,946
Islamic University	697	684	669
King Khalid University	1,755	1,981	1,867
Taibah University	1,546	1,422	1,339
Qassim University	1,804	1,765	1,628
Taif University	1,180	1,142	1,117
Higher education council	25	28	27
Jazan University	1,157	1,095	1,025
ALJouf University	734	723	710
Hail University	874	849	818
Tabuk University	1,363	768	708
AL-Baha University	632	612	555
Najran University	565	514	496
Princess Nora university for girls	2,483	2,401	1,993
AL-Hudoud Alshamalya university	548	520	454

Dammam University	1,983	2,056	1,808
Prince Sattam bin Abdulaziz university	940	911	851
Majmaah University	685	606	601
Shaqra University	812	701	606
Saudi Electronic university	283	276	256
Jeddah university	331	-	-
Hafr Al-Batin University	258	-	-
Bisha University	297	-	-
Technical and Vocational Training Corporation	4,324	4,392	4,374
Public Education Evaluation Commission	38	73	-
Total	182,695	176,451	171,031
Education Projects	32127.778	31160.475	30542.173
Grand Total	214,823	207,612	201,573

Saudis studying abroad

According to the Saudi Statistics Center, the total number of Saudis studying abroad in 2017 was 122,532 students – 85,049 males and 37,483 females. Most of these

Saudis who are studying abroad have a scholarship for the Saudi government to fund their education. The number of students abroad includes all Saudis at all levels in higher education and medical programs. Saudi students in the bachelor stage make up the largest proportion of the number of Saudi students abroad. In 2017, they numbered 67,400 students, and 14,497 of them were females. The number of Saudi students abroad in the master stage was 27589 students, with 14785 of them being males. The total number of doctoral students was 13517, and 5935 students were females.

Summary

This chapter summarized the most critical stages of education in Saudi Arabia and the beginning of formal education. The section also tried to highlight the most prominent features of Saudi education that make it different from many educational systems in the West. For instance, Saudi education is a religious system, not a secular one. In addition, the chapter presented the essential official statistics related to public schools in the Kingdom. The last portion of the chapter discussed higher education in Saudi Arabia as well as Saudis who study abroad.

Chapter Four: Literature on Saudi international students in the United States

Saudi students began studying in American higher education institutions officially in the second half of the 1950s. Nevertheless, the first study on Saudi students in the United States was in 1972 by Abdulrahman Ibrahim Jammaz, who conducted a quantitative dissertation as partial fulfillment of the requirements for the degree of Doctor of Philosophy at Michigan State University. Studies and literature on Saudi students in the United States are limited and very few compared to the research on Asian international students, such as Chinese and Koreans, at American universities. Moreover, the majority of studies on Saudi international students in the United States were doctoral dissertations, not scientific articles published in scientific journals, and that is a significant limitation in the literature on Saudi students in the States.

As I stated earlier, studies on Saudi students began in the early 1970s, which means that the first study on Saudi students was almost half a century ago, and during the past 50 years, the world has witnessed huge political, economic, and technical changes and revolutions that have influenced our contemporary reality. For instance, Saudi-U.S. relations across the past 50 years have gone through some difficult obstacles, especially throughout the 1973 Arab-Israeli war, in which the U.S. government supported Israel over Arabs. This led to a diplomatic and then economic crisis after Saudi Arabia and Arab countries stopped oil exports, causing a global economic crisis. However, the 1973 war was a tiny dilemma compared to the events of 9/11, where a number of perpetrators were Saudis.

The events of 9/11 have greatly affected the reputation of Arabs and Muslims in the world, especially in the West, leading many Westerners and individuals to label Arabs and Muslims as terrorists. Readers of Western books and studies on Saudi Arabia, including Saudi students in the United States, published after the events of 9/11 will observe that such literature devotes a large section to talking about the events of 9/11 in detail because this event had a large impact on many groups around the world, particularly Saudi international students in the United States. The events of 9/11 influenced the Saudis in the United States to a great extent, as well as their expectations and perceptions of the United States, especially before they arrived to the States, as you will read in the studies presented in this chapter. Therefore, I divided the studies on Saudi students into two sections: the first section presents the studies before the 9/11 events and the second section presents those after the 9/11 events.

This chapter shows studies on Saudi international students in the United States. This chapter attempts to present the largest portion of old and new studies on Saudi students in American higher education institutions. It is worth knowing the number of studies on Saudis in the States is limited, and most of these studies are doctorate dissertations. Chapter four is generally divided into two parts, the old and new studies on Saudi students in the

United States. The events of September 11, 2001 changed many circumstances and factors that may have had an impact on the results of the studies on Saudis. As a result, I believe it is wise to divide the studies into two parts.

The first part shows the studies before the terrorist attack, and the second review studies after the events of 9/11. Further, the second part deals with 13 recent studies in detail published in the last ten years.

Readers will notice that the old studies (before 2001) on Saudi students use the quantitative research method, while the majority of recent studies apply qualitative or mixed method research. Before moving on to read the studies on Saudi students, this would be an excellent moment to recall the main distinctions between quantitative and qualitative research. Briefly, quantitative research "is the collection and analysis of numerical data to describe, explain, predict or control phenomena of interest." On the other hand, qualitative research is defined as "the collection, analysis, and interpretation of comprehensive narrative and visual (non numerical data) to gain insight into a particular phenomenon of interest" (Gay, Mills, & Airasian, 2012, p. 7). Mixed methods research is simply a methodology for conducting research that involves collecting, analyzing, and integrating quantitative and qualitative research.

QUALITATIVE VERSUS QUANTITATIVE RESEARCH

QUALITATIVE VERSUS QUANTITATIVE RESEARCH

*souce: (Johnson, & Christensen, 2008, Lichtman,2006; xavier Uni, 2012)

Criteria	Quantitative Research	Qualitative Research
Purpose	To test hypotheses, look at cause & effect, & make predictions.	To understand & interpret social interactions.
Participants and sample	Larger & randomly selected.	Smaller & not randomly selected.
Variables	Specific variables studied	Specific variables studied
Type of Data Collected	Numbers and statistics.	Words, images, or objects

Type of Data Analysis		Identify statistical relationships	Identify patterns, features, themes
Objectivity and Subjectivity		Objectivity is critical.	Subjectivity is expected.
Role of Researcher		Researcher & their biases are not known to participants in the study, & participant characteristics are deliberately hidden from the researcher (double blind studies).	Researcher & their biases may be known to participants in the study, & participant characteristics may be known to the researcher.
Results		Generalizable findings that can be applied to other populations.	specialized findings that is less generalizable.
	Most Common	Describe, explain, & predict.	Explore, discover, & construct.
Nature of Observation		Study behavior under controlled conditions; isolate causal effects	Study behavior in a natural environment.

Final Report	Statistical report with correlations, comparisons of means, & statistical significance of findings.	Narrative report with contextual description & direct quotations from research participants.

Selections of old studies on Saudis in the United States Before 9/11

The majority of the studies on Saudi students in U.S. higher education were conducted before the 9/11 terrorist event, which may impact the reputation of Saudi students negatively (Akhtarkhavari, 1994; Alfauzan, 1992; Al-Ghamdi, 1985; AlHarthi, 1987; Al-Jasir, 1993; Al-Khedaire, 1978; Al-nusair, 2000; Al-Shedokhi, 1986;Al-Shehry, 1989; El-Banyan, 1974; Jammaz, 1972; Mustafa, 1985; Oweidat, 1981; Shabeeb, 1996). It is noteworthy that studies on Saudi students in the United States were all doctoral dissertations and not studies published in scientific journals. Doctoral dissertations on Saudi students pre-9/11 almost all use the quantitative method. Additionally, several of the researchers were applying Michigan International Students Problem Inventory (MISPI). The MISPI measure was developed by Porter (1966) in 1962; it was revised in 1977 and consists of a total of 132 items partitioned into eleven subscales that assess different adjustment problem areas encountered by international students. The subscales (problem areas) include: (a) admission-selection, (b) orientation service, (c) academic record, (d) social-personal, (e) living-dining, (f) health service, (g) religious service, (h) English language, (i) student activity, (j) financial aid, and (k) placement service (Can, 2015, p. 87).

Abdulrahman Ibrahim Jammaz was the first researcher who conducted a study on Saudi international students in the United States in 1972. Jammaz conducted quantitative dissertation at Michigan State University, and the title of this dissertation was Saudi students in the United States: a study of their adjustment problems. Jammaz surveyed 345 Saudi Arabian students studying in different higher education institutions in the States. He found that younger students were less well adjusted than older students, married students were less well adjusted than unmarried students, and those majoring in the humanities and social science were less well adjusted than students majoring in science and engineering. Jammaz also concluded that students who had not been employed before arriving in the United States were more adjusted than students who had been employed. Jammaz also noticed there was a low correlation between length of stay in the U.S. and adjustment. He added that many students reported having problems with English experiencing difficulties with writing which was the biggest obstacle for Saudis. At the Same time, Saudis experienced difficulties with reading, taking notes and participating in class discussions. Further, he discovered that the Saudi students who had the highest connection, and were socialization with Americans, had the highest degree of adjustment. This association with Americans also had a significant positive effect on academic achievement.

Kershaw (1973 as cited in Caldwell, 2013) examined Saudi Arabian attitudes toward religion in the state of Oregon and found that Saudi Arabian students tended to be less faithful in observing Muslim rules for fasting and prayer while in the United States. Also, participants reported no extensive contact with religious Americans, did not attend non-Muslim religious services, and were generally uncertain as to how to view Christianity. A significant finding of the research was that despite a decrease in strict observance, the students became more committed to Islam and Islamic values after moving to Oregon.

Al-Khedairy, in his dissertation conducted at the University of Arizona in 1978, studied Saudi male students' perceptions and attitudes toward American culture and people. 300 Saudi Arabian students in the United States were divided into three groups according to the length of their stay in the country. The quantitative study found that the length of sojourn was not a contributing factor to attitude differences among the Saudi Arabian students toward the host country. Al-Khedairy also noticed that students majoring in science showed a clearer perception of United States culture than students majoring in social sciences or related fields did, and graduate students showed a clearer cultural perception of the host nation than the undergraduate students did. Also, the researcher stated that any previous international contact of the students before arriving in the United States had no effect on either their cultural perception or attitude toward the host nation. The study also concluded that socioeconomic status had no effect on either the cultural perception or the attitude toward the United States by Saudi Arabian students in the United States, and marital status was not a contributing factor to significant differences in either cultural perceptions or attitudes of the participants toward the host country. The researcher found students in small colleges indicated a more positive attitude toward the United States than those in larger academic institutions.

In 1985 Mustafa completed his dissertation titled Saudi students in the United States: A study of their adjustment problems. He conducted quantitative research surveying 47 Saudi Arabian students, 22 instructors, 24 administrators at Western Michigan University, and 8 academic advisors from the Saudi Arabian cultural Mission. Mustafa found English was the main academic challenge for Saudi students. Mustafa's study connected the amount of time a Saudi student spends in the United States to enhanced language fluency; accordingly, the researcher noted that Saudi students who spent less time in the United States had more problems in English skills, and, he added students who had shorter sojourns perceived more problems in the areas of writing essay exams, taking notes, understanding the American educational system, and having too many credit hours of study in one semester. Mustafa concluded that the amount of time spent in the United States did not influence students adjustment.

Al-Shehry (1989) surveyed 354 graduate students using the MISPI to find the concerns of Saudi students. in the USA. The researcher found one of the areas considered the greatest concern to Saudi students was financial aid and using English in, for example, writing essays, and academic records such as grades. He concluded that Saudis who study in American universities not only need to be able to read and write in academic English for schoolwork, but they must also understand expressions, slang, humor, dialects, and jokes in daily interactions in order to function in everyday life in the United States. He found that giving oral presentations, understanding lectures, taking notes, participating in discussions, writing essays and papers, and speaking to fellow students and professors were also challenging aspects for most Saudi students. Al-Shehry found that Saudis experienced being discriminated against, especially with respect to the grades they received in comparison to their American classmates. Finally, the researcher found that the Saudi participants believed that the US media depicts Saudi Arabia and Saudis wrongly and negatively, which led many locals to have negative stereotypes of Saudi Arabia and its citizens.

Shabeeb (1996 as cited in Aldossari, 2016) conducted research to explore the factors that may affect both Saudi and other international students from the Arabian Gulf in the United States. The sample included 150 international students (male and female) attending six colleges and universities in eastern Washington. The results show the adjustment problems of these international students from most severe to least difficult: (a) language barriers, (b) social-personal issues, (c) living-dining problems, (d) grades, (e) orientation service, (f) admission, (g) placement service, (h) student activities, (i) religious service, (j) health service, and (k) financial aid.

Al-Nusair (2000 as cited in Al-Romahe, 2018) used the College Student Experiences Questionnaire to measure the amount of effort Saudi students devote to using the facilities and the opportunities for learning and development that university campuses offer them. The 171 Saudi Arabian international students who participated in the study were more likely to use campus resources and activities that were geared toward learning such as the library, opportunities for conversation, and interaction with faculty. They were less likely to engage in activities and resources that were oriented toward entertainment and socialization such as clubs, student organizations, music, writing, art, and theatre (p.71). Al-Nusair (2000) advised that international student offices find techniques to help Saudi international students to engage in more university-sponsored social events to create supportive connections within the community, help Saudi students adjust to the new culture, address feelings of isolation and homesickness, and minimize experiences with discrimination and lack of belonging. Al-Nusair's study differs from the current research in that it is very broad and not focused on the student-teacher relationship, and it is based on quantitative analysis and doesn't reflect the nuanced experiences of the Saudi students.

Selections of studies on Saudis in the United States after 9/11

Several changes have occurred since the studies presented above were written. Among these changes, as a result of the 9/11 tragedy, the intercultural communication between Saudi and American students was especially affected (Al Musaiteer, 2015). Fifteen out of nineteen of the hijackers responsible for the 9/11 tragedy were Saudis. Accordingly, the way that Americans perceive and treat Saudi students has changed dramatically since the 9/11 event (Al Musaiteer, 2015). Some Saudi students experienced discrimination, alienation, and fear (Ghaffari, 2009). Some Saudi students did not complete their studies and left the USA immediately after the tragedy, and others changed the way they looked, such as women removing their headscarves and men shaving their beards (McMurtrie et al., 2001).

Consequently, it would be beneficial to concentrate more on recent dissertations and articles on Saudis that were published after the September 11 event. This section presents ten dissertations and three journal articles on Saudi Arabian international students in the United States that have been published in the past ten years. This part attempts to display the information in a simple way, using bulleted lists. All recent studies on Saudi international students have applied qualitative or mixed methods, which means the numbers of participants were lower than in the studies conducted before 2001. Nevertheless, qualitative research provides in-depth information that makes the reader understand the results.

Study 1

The Title of the study: **The Identification of Issues Serving as Barriers to Positive Educational Experiences for Saudi Arabian Students Studying in the State of Missouri**			
The Researcher name:	Jean Hofer	University	University of Missouri - Saint Louis
Year of study:	2009	Type of research	Dissertations
Research methodology	mixed method approach	The Instruments for data collection	MISPI & interviews
Number of participants	81 participants Saudi studying in Missouri.		

Significant findings

1. Younger students encountered more adjustment difficulties compared to older students in the social-personal category.

2. Single students experienced more difficulties in the English language, social-personal, and admission-selection categories than married students.

3. The participants who had lived in the United States for two years or less experienced more problems in the English language and living-dining categories than the participants who had lived in the United States for a longer time.

4. Participants reported minor problems; the essential challenges included living and dining issues, English language obstacles, and financial aid concerns.

5. Saudi males faced more adjustment problems than females in some areas of academic life in the U.S.

6. Participants attending smaller-sized colleges (10,000 students or less) experienced fewer obstacles in the English language category than those attending larger institutions.

7. Generally, Saudi students in the state of Missouri were satisfied with their educational experiences.

8. The researcher found that Saudi participants had fewer adjustment challenges than Saudi or Arabian students who were studied previously.

Study 2

The Title of the study: **Bridging Differences: Saudi Arabian Students Reflect on Their Educational Experiences and Share Success Strategies**			
The Researcher name:	Donna L. Shaw	University	Oregon State University
Year of study:	2009	Type of research	dissertation
Research methodology	Qualitative	The Instruments for data collection	She used three types of interviews: semi-structured, photo-elicitation, and focus groups.
Number of participants	25 Saudi participants, 7 women, and 18 men		

Significant findings

1. This study concentrated on the differences between the home educational environment and the American educational environments for a group of Saudi students.

2. The study reported that the participants found significant differences between the educational environment between Saudi Arabia and America regarding the role of students in class and the issue of attendance.

3. Instructors in Saudi Arabia tend to be more flexible than Americans when it comes to accepting their students' excuses if they are absent or do not complete assignments on time.

4. One example of the differences between Saudi Arabia and the United States educational setting that the participants mentioned was the presence of the opposite sex in U.S. classrooms, including teachers and classmates.

5. Participants reported that technology has a much stronger presence in the US than it has in their Saudi schools.

6. One noticeable difference between Saudi Arabia and the United States was the weather. Most Saudis saw snow for the first time in their lives in the USA.

7. Another example of the remarkable cultural differences between Saudi Arabia and the United States for the Saudis was the presence of Christianity and the almost complete absence of Islam in Oregon. For many participants, they saw churches for the first time in their lives in the USA because there are no churches in Saudi Arabia yet.

8. Participants reported having difficulties with English, adjustment, managing full-time study in a foreign language, and homesickness.

9. Personal adaptation resilience and intercultural competence were the most fundamental characteristics for the Saudi students to be successful in American higher education settings.

10. The researcher advised supporting resilience and intercultural competence by helping Saudi students develop and enhance their coping skills and offering assistance that improves intercultural competence.

11. My participants reported that American classroom practices—which include active classrooms, pair work, group work, projects, papers, frequent quizzes and exams, required attendance, constant homework, and self directed learning—and culture to be elements of their new environment that were different, sometimes challenging, and often marginalizing. (P. 225)

12. Shaw found that the Saudi students developed success strategies,:

    a. Time management and goal setting,

b. Developing and using study skills
   c. Forming study groups
   d. Taking advantage of campus resources
   e. Working hard and persisting
   f. Interacting with other students/cultures (P.229)

13. The participants also shared success strategies including:
    A. Giving opinions about professors and recommending classes
    B. Attending all classes
    C. Getting advice for listening and speaking from teachers
    D. Managing time
    E. Studying hard Getting good study materials/books for the GRE, TOEFL
    F. Spending free time in the Learning Center
    G. Asking for writing help from the free tutors in the Learning Center
    H. Doing homework Using good reading strategies
    I. Making good notes for the TOEFL speaking section

J. Watching the time when taking the TOEFL Including an introduction, body and conclusion in the writing sections of the TOEFL. (P.230)

Study 3

The Title of the study:			
AN EXPLORATION OF THE CASE OF SAUDI STUDENTS' ENGAGEMENT, SUCCESS, AND SELF-EFFICACY AT A MID WESTERN AMERICAN UNIVERSITY			
The Researcher name:	Abdel Nasser Abdel Razek	University	University of Akron
Year of study:	2012	Type of research	Dissertation
Research methodology	qualitative	The Instruments for data collection	interviews
Number of participants	11 Saudi students including female and male, one professor, and one administrator.		

Chosen Direct Quotations

> The collectivistic thinking of Saudi students causes them to think of themselves as a group rather than a number of individuals. Such consideration, though positive in nature, increases the boundaries between the Saudi students as a group and the rest of the student body at RSU. Ahmed states, "If I hang with other students, they are usually Saudi. They are a lot here now. I did not expect to see many of them and they were not as much when I arrived. I feel more comfortable with them than with American friends. We speak the same language and talk about the same things." Another challenge that faces Saudi students is making new friends with American students. The degree of connectedness of Saudi students sometimes hinders their ability to socialize and build new social relationships outside of their group. (p.97)

> However, their academic preparedness is always questioned by their professors. Hanan expresses how difficult it was to read and study in English when she first arrived in the United States. She says, "I came here after the secondary school … I always had English as a school subject but the English we studied is different than the one we see spoken here. The books are also very difficult and have lots of words and abbreviations that I am not used to read. I always find it very difficult." Jehad also expresses how his studies differed here and in Saudi Arabia. He says, "I studied for one year in college… but I studied business in Arabic. … Now, I am learning it

in English, which makes it a problem for me. I am also not comfortable to write papers in English. ... This is always my biggest problem. I did not even use to write papers in Arabic. We usually study and then have tests at the end of the year." Zeyad also expresses how his expectations of his college study were far from reasonable. "I did not imagine the amount of reading that professors want us to read. I have to read more than four hundred pages each week to prepare for my classes. At the beginning of the semester, I thought I can read that much. Now, I usually try to read the major points and get the class notes of other students who took the class before," he says. Therefore, one major transition challenge for Saudi students is their language proficiency. At RSU, like any other American institutions, Saudi students deal with textbooks written in English as the language of classroom instruction. If their language proficiency level is low, then it is logical that their academic performance reflects that deficiency. (p. 105)

Significant findings

1. The study found that generally Saudi students come to the United States with high expectations of an elite college education to match their perception of an ideal college experience because Saudi students believe that the US has the best higher education system. This conclusion agrees with almost all studies on Saudi students in the United States.

2. Not mastering the English language was a major academic obstacle for Saudi students.

3. Saudi students also face difficulty with teaching methods, the number of assignments, and teachers' expectations.

4. The study mentioned that Saudi participants defined their success by the degrees that they had earned. A few of these Saudis perceived success in their experience as a whole and how they learned more about other cultures, in addition to the degree.

5. The participants experienced many stereotypes about their religion, ethnic group, and country.

6. Participants reported that the media create distorted perceptions about Saudi Arabia.

7. Social integration with Americans was met with many obstacles like religious difference, the mixed gender aspect of American culture, and dietary restrictions. The Saudi participants, as Muslims, did not drink alcohol nor eat pork, and the female students wore the hijab.

Study 4

The Title of the study:

EXAMINING THE EXPERIENCES AND ADJUSTMENT CHALLENGES OF SAUDI ARABIAN STUDENTS IN THE CALIFORNIA STATE UNIVERSITY SYSTEM				
The Researcher name:	Jeremy Dean Caldwell	University	California State University, Fresno
Year of study:	2013	Type of research	dissertation
Research methodology	Mixed method study (both quantitative and qualitative methods)	The Instruments for data collection	1-MISPI test to collect quantitative data,. 2- focus group sessions to collect the qualitative data

Chosen Direct Quotations

Some Saudi Arabian students have experienced discrimination from workers in the local communities. Some of these incidents have been somewhat concealed such as car dealers raising the prices of automobiles after learning that a student was from Saudi Arabia, to workers in restaurants not giving quality service to Saudi Arabians. However, others occurrences have been more explicit. A student from San Jose State reported an instance at a train station when a worker directly inquired of the student's nationality. When the student revealed his nationality, the worker said, "Do you have a gun? Do you have a bomb?" The student believed that the reason this man said this was because of the stereotypes typically associated with Saudi Arabians. (p. 148)

Saudi Arabian students also claimed to experience discrimination on campus. Although most of the respondents reported no instances of discrimination on campus, some revealed that instances of discrimination came about from professors and teachers as well as from fellow classmates. Participants from three campuses expressed feeling as though professors and teachers preferred Chinese or Japanese students to them, and stated that despite raised hands, professors and teachers would not call on them in class. In addition, one student claimed that an English professor accused him of cheating by turning in a paper that was not his. The student expressed frustration over the professor singling him out in front of the entire class. Another student was embarrassed when a teacher jokingly asked if he came to America on a camel, and two students expressed feeling picked on by teachers.(p. 151)

These students revealed problems renting homes. They indicated that some property owners would not rent to them, and others simply raised the prices after learning of the students' nationality. Although the federal Fair Housing Act prohibits property owners from choosing renters based on variables such as race, nationality or religion, Saudi Arabian students in California have experienced these types of discriminatory acts against them. This finding may be attributed to Americans' fear, suspicion, and/or hatred of people from the Middle East. (p. 169)

Significant findings

1. A modified version of the Michigan International Student Problem Inventory (MISPI) was employed at ten California State University (CSU) campuses to determine the adjustment problems of Saudi Arabian students.

2. Participants in the study included 276 Saudi students divided into two groups by data collection type. The first group of 245 students completed the survey (quantitative section), and in group two there were 31 students divided into five focus groups (the qualitative section).

3. The Saudi participants ordered their issues from those of most concern to those of least

concern according to the MISPI categories. These rankings are as follows: Admission-Selection, Social-Personal, Academic Record, Living-Dining, Placement Service, English Language, Student Activities, Health Service, Orientation Service, and Religious Service.

4. One of the most critical point this study discovered Saudi students in the CSU ranked English to be as the sixth-most-problematic for them, and that result is different from previous research on Saudi students in the US, that used the same test (MISPI). According to Al-Shehry (1989), Mustafa (1985), and Shabeeb (1996), English was the most challenging adjustment encountered for Saudis, and Hofer (2009) found English was the second-most-difficult. However, data from participants of focus groups (qualitative section) placed English issues as the topmost problem that Saudi students met in the US.

5. Saudi students were generally pleased with their lives in California.

6. The majority of Saudi students in the CSU experienced discrimination.

7. This study showed that Saudi Arabian students experienced little to no problems adjusting to life in California.

8. Saudi students believed that they are more religious than are Americans.

9. Saudis had problems with homesickness and developing friendships with Americans.

10. Saudi students expressed challenges with strict attendance policies at American universities.

11. Saudi participants at CSU also indicated that the CSU's admission requirements were rigorous. Participants were mainly frustrated with the high scores needed on English assessments such as the TOEFL and IELTS, as well as with graduate admissions tests such as the Graduate Record Examination (GRE) and the Graduate Management Admission Test (GMAT).

12. The findings identified that age and having or not having children did not significantly affect student adjustment in the CSU system.

13. Male students encountered greater difficulties with the Academic Records category than did female students.

14. The study also found females had more problems with recurrent headaches and feelings of tension than did male students.

15. Single students faced more academic challenges compared to married students.

16. Most participants believed that their relationships with their professors and instructors were good and positive.

Study 5

The Title of the study: **Experiences of Male Saudi Arabian International Students in the United States**			
The Researcher name:	Molly Elizabeth Heyn	University	Western Michigan University
Year of study:	2013	Type of research	dissertation
Research methodology	qualitative study	The Instruments for data collection	semi structured interviews
Number of participants	9 male Saudi Arabian international college students		

Significant findings

1. The Saudi participants had positive and negative perceptions and expectations prior to studying in the United States; the positive side is that the U.S. has a strong higher education system that has a good reputation around the globe and that offers advanced technology. On the other hand, participants believed that the USA was an unsafe country to live in, and Americans would not treat Saudis nicely.

2. The Saudi participants in this study stated some changes in their perceptions after having lived and studied in the United States, such as that the U.S. people were friendlier than they perceived prior to studying in the United States and that the United States was safer than they thought prior to their arrival.

3. English was the major academic obstacle for Saudi students participating in this study.

4. Many participants felt embarrassed when speaking in English in front of students and instructors because they believed they did not speak fluent English.

5. Missing their families and friends and homesickness were common personal challenges among the participants.

6. The Saudi participants expressed concern for letting family members and their government down as a primary motivator to succeed in their academic journey in the United States.

7. The support services that participants sought and received during their time in the United States included help from professors, reliance on their religion, and support from their families and other Saudi Arabian students.

8. The participants wished to complete their study programs and return to Saudi Arabia to contribute to the development of their society and their country.

9. After studying in the United States, the participants thought that their notions about the role of women in society have become more positive than before, and the participants believed in the importance of empowering women in the Saudi society.

10. Studying in the United States was an opportunity for the participants to be open to cultures, and through participation, they became more respectful of other cultures.

11. Some participants disliked the weather in the Midwestern region of the United States due to cold, while simultaneously missing the weather in their home country.

12. Saudi participants believe they have been able to correct many of the Americans' mistaken and negative beliefs about Saudi Arabia and the Saudis.

13. Part of the Saudi participants experienced racism and prejudice while studying in the United States.

Study 6

The Title of the study: **EXPERIENCES OF SAUDI STUDENTS ATTENDING A U.S. UNIVERSITY: A QUALITATIVE STUDY**			
The Researcher name:	Hala Y. Alsabatin	University	Wichita State University
Year of study:	2015	Type of research	Dissertation
Research methodology	QUALITATIVE	The Instruments for data collection	interviews
Number of participants	\multicolumn{3}{l	}{The data were collected using individual interviews with 21 Saudi students who were}

	undergraduate and graduate students (seven female and 14 male).

Chosen Direct Quotations

Duration of stay in the United States affected the Saudis' full integration. While living and studying in the U.S., Saudi participants explored the acculturation strategies and changed their acculturation preferences to meet their needs. Even though most participants preferred integration, they were more likely to change their strategy when they were about to leave the U.S. To illustrate, most undergraduate participants were eager and enthusiastic to be integrated because they knew they would spend a long period living and studying in the U.S. Yet, some graduate Saudi male and female participants, when they felt their duration of stay in the U.S. would be short and about to end, tended to reduce their interactions with Americans and chose the separation strategy. They attributed the reason to being busy with their academic studies and family matters. Thus, the Saudis' desire for integration in the host culture was noticed in the initial stages of their living in the U.S. culture, but then started to diminish. In contrast, immigrants' length of residence is in a positive relationship with their desire to be integrated in the mainstream culture. (P 115)

Significant findings

1. The researcher divided the results into two parts. The first section concerned the analysis of the information collected from the female participants, while the other section was for male participants.

2. The researcher justified the division of the results by gender because of the differences between males and females in Islamic society. For example, according to Saudi cultural norms and Islamic religious rules, female Saudi students are not allowed to live abroad alone, so they must be accompanied by a husband or "mahram". (mahram means a male guardian in Arabic)

3. The seven female participants shared similar aims and reasons for studying abroad and chose the United States specifically to pursue their higher education due to limited options for majors available at universities in Saudi Arabia, dissatisfaction with the Saudi higher educational system, and having a mahram who was already studying in the U.S.

4. The seven female participants felt they had become more independent and self-confident after moving to the United States.

5. The seven female members of the study in the United States found an opportunity to interact with the students of the local and foreign communities and the American community, which helped them to learn about American culture and cultural openness.

6. Some participants do not speak fluent English, which negatively affects their interaction with American women.

7. Female participants often speak with female American women and prefer not talking to men for cultural reasons.

8. Most of the female participants were satisfied with the way their American teachers and advisors treated them.

9. Female participants faced academic difficulties because of their poor English skills and felt that they had not well prepared in the Language Institute before entering the university.

10. Generally, male participants were less constrained by religion and culture than female participants. Accordingly, their acculturation experiences were distinct from those of the females as their integration was affected by the host culture.

11. Most female and male participants wanted to interact with the Americans because interaction with students and the local

community are essential to learn about American culture and improve the English skills of the participants.

12. The participants found difficulties in forming friendships and relationships with Americans, which discouraged participants from interacting with local students and the community.

13. The majority of the female participants said they did not favor frequent interaction with male students for cultural and religious reasons. Furthermore, most of the female participants described having even more space and boundaries with Saudi male students than with American male students.

14. Some female participants expected to face intolerance and racism because they wore headscarves. However, the participants were not exposed to any racist attitudes or hatred because of their Islamic appearance, and participants were appropriately treated by professors and local students.

15. The central reason for male participants to study abroad was getting full scholarships from the King Abdullah Scholarship Program (KSAP) to study abroad so the students did not have to worry about financial problems.

16. Some male participants chose to study abroad because they did not have the opportunity to be admitted to the schools or majors they wanted at Saudi universities.

17. Two primary reasons encouraged Saudi male participants to pursue their higher education in the United States, among other developed countries. The first reason was having a family member who had studied or was studying in the United States. The second main reason was the policies and directives of the KASP because Saudis got the scholarship from the KSAP faster when studying in the United States compared to other countries.

18. Most male Saudi participants preferred working with American students in a study group rather than with Saudi classmates.

19. Although they were not directly exposed to racism, many Saudi male participants believed that Americans, both on campus and off it, classify and stereotype Saudis as terrorists. Saudi male participants thought they were subjected to discrimination, stigma, and prejudice because of the terrorist attacks of 9/11.

20. Saudis' inability to speak English fluently was their main restraint to succeeding academically as well as being culturally integrated into the American host culture.

21. Most participants believed that the language institute they studied at was insufficiently preparing them for the appropriate level of English proficiency needed for college courses.

22. Saudi male and female participants shared that the most significant resources for the integration with Americans and participants were living in the university dorms, living with American families and attending non-classroom student activities, which are important for integrating with the host culture.

23. Some participants reported missing the social and emotional support commonly provided by their family members.

Study 7

The Title of the study: **The Cultural Adjustment of Saudi Women International Students: A Qualitative Examination**				
The Researcher name:	Lefdahl-Davis, E. M., & Perrone-McGovern, K. M.			
Year of study:	2015		Type of research	scientific article

Research methodology	Qualitative	The Instruments for data collection	Interviews and surveys
Number of participants	25 Saudi women international students		

The findings were divided into seven themes:

1: Expectations and Reality

2: Culture Shock and Cultural Adjustment

3: Cultural Differences Between Saudi Arabia and United States

4: Experiences of Discrimination and/or Curiosity

5: English Proficiency or Barrier

6: Relationships, Social Support, and Help-Seeking Behavior in the United States

7: Being a Saudi Woman in the United States

Significant findings

1. The first theme showed the difference between the expectations of 25 Saudi female participants before coming to the United States and the reality as experienced after living and studying in the United States.

2. Many Saudi students had expectations about the United States from: movies, television, the internet, or other forms of media.

3. The study found that the participants had expectations of the United States that did not match the reality, such as the United States being an unsafe country where gangs and killings are as portrayed in Hollywood movies, as well as intolerance and racism against Muslims. However, these expectations differed from the reality where the participants found that after living in the United States, the American people were tolerant and friendly and that the United States is a secure country and not as presented in cinemas.

4. Some of the participants' expectations were identical to reality, especially those who have visited other countries before coming to the United States or have friends who study in the United States.

5. One thing to note is that the study found that most Saudi participants do not think they were culturally

shocked or felt acculturative stress when they came to the United States. The reason is that the participants mentioned they traveled to other countries before coming to the United States or they discovered the American culture from different sources, such as asking people who visited the country and checking the internet.

6. Although some Saudi participants said they were subjected to discrimination because of the hijab and Islamic dress, the majority were not exposed to discrimination during their experience in the United States.

7. The researchers stressed that there is a difference between previous studies on international female students in the United States and Saudi international female students in terms of loneliness and social support. Female Saudi students are usually studying in the U.S. with some of their family members, and most of the participants in this study were married. Therefore, it is useful to perceive the cultural differences between international students because the differences are vast in the family and social aspects. For illustration, in the previous literature, international students studying in the United States live alone, without their families, but it is different from Saudi female students, who are required by Saudi regulations to come to the U.S. with a male member of their family, such as a husband or brother.

8. Most of the participants agreed that the English language was a primary part of their adjustment to

the United States, and half of the participants reported that they speak English fluently.

9. The majority of participants said studying in the United States was a life-changing experience, and they became more independent, confident, and open to other cultures.

Study 8

The Title of the study:

A narrative inquiry into academic experiences of female Saudi graduate students at a comprehensive doctoral university. *Journal of Studies in International*			
The Researcher names:	Sandekian, R. E., Weddington, M., Birnbaum, M., & Keen, J. K.		
Year of Publication	2015	Type of research	Journal Article
Research methodology	Qualitative	The Instruments for data collection	Interviews
Number of participants	4 Saudi Arabian female graduate students at a college of education in a university in the Western part of the US.		

The findings were divided into four themes:

- A-Language Challenges

- B-Interactions With Men
- C-Interactions With Faculty
- D-Academic and Lived Experiences

Significant findings

1. The researcher focused on two main topics in the literature review section. First, it has focused on the increasing number of Saudi students in American universities in recent years due to the Saudi government scholarship program (King Abdullah External Scholarship Program). The previous literature section also focuses on cultural differences in the study environments between Saudi Arabia and the United States, because in Saudi Arabia there is gender separation in all public places including university campuses and classrooms.

2. English was the main challenge in their programs for female Saudi students.

3. The information provided by the study showed that the participants presented the following views regarding the difficulties facing them during graduate studies.

4. Saudi students faced difficulties completing some assignments due to language challenges.

5. Writing academically was a challenge for these Saudis.

6. Saudi students felt that their English abilities affected their academic achievement.

7. Saudi students faced challenges understanding their teachers and other local students because they spoke fast and used informal words like idioms.

8. The participants believed that it would help if the instructors could spend more time explaining concepts and Saudi spent more time in ESL programs to master English skills.

9. Saudi female participants had different perceptions of the study than Saudi male students. According to the study, some female participants prefer not to study with male Saudi colleagues in the same classes because those males try to impose their power over the females. Also, one participant stated that Saudi males did not let females speak freely and without interruption with their professors and other classmates. At the same time, participants generally had no issues with interacting and studying with male American classmates.

10. In general, the Saudi female participants had a good impression of all their professors and did not mind working and studying with their male professors.

11. The participants also described their American professors as kind, tolerant, and culturally aware.

Study 9

The Title of the study: **Factors Contributing to College Retention of Undergraduate Saudi Students Studying in the United States**			
The Researcher name:	Abdulaziz Salem Aldossari	University	The University of Wisconsin-Milwaukee,
Year of study:	2016	Type of research	Dissertation
Research methodology	**Mixed methods research**	The Instruments for data collection	
Number of participants	45 Saudi undergraduate students from three different universities in the State of Wisconsin		

Chosen Direct Quotations

The survey results demonstrate the patterns of factors affecting Saudi students in completing their bachelor degree in the U.S. from most severe to least: (a) Personal Factor, (b) Psychological Factor, (c) Faculty Factor, (d) Engagement Factor, (e) University Services Factor, and (f) Financial factors. (p.140)

The expectations parents have for the education of their children was associated with the students' motivation to complete their education abroad. Both survey and interview analysis conclude that father's education level were endorsed by participants as important contributors to motivating their degree completion, which was considered a Personal factor. In other words, students whose fathers have a high level degree tend to persist more than those whose fathers have low degree.(p.141)

All participants reported that they appreciated the institutional resources, services, and activities while attempting to complete their degree. Tutoring and writing centers help the students with their academic challenges, which eventually ensures their academic adjustment and retention. Academic services and entertainment facilities help the students to be more engaged socially as well as academically. The finding shows that female students had different perspectives than males regarding university activities and facilities. They reported that they cannot engage such activities as gyms because of the mixing of genders that entails. 143 Based on that, these students might appreciate facilities that meet and respect their cultural and religious concepts..(p.143)

Significant findings

1. Firstly, the researcher surveyed 45 students. Then, he conducted face-to-face interviews with 10 of those students to gain a descriptive depth of information.

2. Psychological and financial factors were more effective motivators for married students than single students concerning the completion of their degrees.

3. Participants whose fathers hold a two-year college degree had the highest mean toward their completion of the bachelor's degree, whereas the lowest mean was registered with the father's partial completion of some college educational level.

4. English deficiency was not a barrier for the participants that led them to quit collegiate education in the US.

5. Participants aimed to complete their bachelor's degree to gain a better prospective career or attain a better social standing (social class) in their society when they came back to their country.

6. The participants viewed their high self-efficacy and self-esteem as elemental in the successful completion of their degrees.

7. Participants provided positive answers toward their interaction with their faculty and academic advisors.

8. The participants encountered cultural difficulties in the United States; however, these challenges can be overcome.

9. Participants considered the Saudi government financial aid a positive motivation toward completing their bachelor's diploma in the United States.

10. Because the participants already obtained scholarships with a fully paid tuition as well as a monthly salary, they would not see finances as a major obstacle.

Study 10

The Title of the study: **Saudi International University Students' Perceptions of Their Relationships with American Teachers at a Large Western Research University**			
The Researcher name:	Mohamed Al-Romahe	University	Doctor of Education in Curriculum and Instruction. Boise State University
Year of study:	2018	Type of research	dissertation
Research methodology	Qualitative	The Instruments for data collection	Interviews

Number of participants	5 male Saudi students at a large Western research university

Significant findings

1. Saudi participants said it is essential for them that their American professors know their names and information about them. However, the participants reported that most professors do not even know their names, which causes a weakness in the relationship between Saudi students and their instructors at American universities.

2. The Saudi participants believe that being seen and understood by their professors was a primary factor in their academic as well as social success.

3. The Saudis stated that being recognized as Saudi learners without awareness and knowledge of their culture can lead to stereotyping and negative judgments.

4. The five Saudis noticed these differences between the expected roles of students and instructors to be a cause of misinterpretation. The participants have discovered that what is considered respect in Saudi Arabia is often considered to be a lack of participation or incompetence in the U.S. classroom. Participant 2 stated:in Saudi culture, students tend to be quiet in class, and making eye contact with teachers is considered inappropriate; however, he

feels his teachers at the American university judge him poorly for what is considered a sign of respect in Saudi Arabian classrooms. American teachers value classroom discussion and view students' participation as a sign of competence, but in Saudi classrooms, students are not expected to participate. (p. 51).

5. The Saudis said that they had difficulties communicating with their teachers and hardness reading and writing because these Saudis struggle with English abilities.

6. Participants found it difficult to understand lectures when their professors speak fast.

7. Visual aids such as photos and PowerPoint presentations helped participants understand lessons better.

8. Participants agreed that the academic services and campus resource provided by the University such as the Writing Center that helps students with editing their papers was essential to their education.

9. The participants also faced difficulties to communicate with their American classmates, and the participants felt that the Americans did not want to make friendships with the Saudis. Participants noted difficulties in communicating not only with their teachers but with their classmates. They expressed their experiences of feeling isolated from other classmates and how they see the educator's role in improving relationships

among students. Participant #4 said, "It's not only the teacher who doesn't know who I am, but also, my classmates, some of my classmates don't understand why I come here to study. One of my classmates asked me 'don't you have colleges?'" Saudi students want to be recognized by other students as well as the teacher, and feel the teacher should play a role. (P. 57)

10. "The participants' experience was that Saudi international students have been stereotyped as cheaters, which makes them feel disconnected and places them in a position of marginalization and neglect within the classroom." (p. 52)

Study 11

The Title of the study: **Collectivists' Decision-Making: Saudi Arabian Graduate Students' Study Abroad Choices**			
The Researcher names:	1. Tamara Yakaboski 2. Karla Perez-Velez 3. Yousef Almutairi		University of Northern Colorado, USA
Year of study:	2017	Type of research	Peer-Reviewed Article, published in Journal of International Students, 7(1) 2017

Research methodology	qualitative	The Instruments for data collection	Semi-structured interviews
Number of participants	18 Saudi graduate students, 14 men and 4 women. All were on full scholarship from the government, and all were studied at one mid-sized research university in the Western region of the United States.		

Significant findings

1. The researchers found that one of the most important factors that attract Saudis to study in America is the reputation of American higher education, which was considered by the participants the best in the world, and the quality of the academic output of American universities. One participant stated: It was my dream to come here and study in the USA. I found the USA [degree] is, like, more valuable in Saudi Arabia. That study in the USA is more valuable because it [is from a] very good university, very high-ranking university and a good community, a good educational system here in USA so that's why they [SACM] encourage us to come to the USA. (p. 101)

2. Learning English as the language of science and the language of the world at present also motivates the Saudis to study in the United States.

3. One of the reasons that Saudi graduate students leave their country to go to the United States was that there were not enough graduate programs suitable for their academic majors in Saudi universities.

4. "Participants viewed U.S. graduate education as an opportunity to develop KSA educational systems and knowledge. The participants were aware that they were helping to grow and improve Saudi higher education programs through their transnational temporary migration". (p. 103)

5. Saudi participants have shown no interest in and do not care about the ranking of the universities at which they study, and they describe university classifications as inaccurate and unrealistic like this participant: For my personal point of view about rankings, I don't care what's the rank of the university, or whatever, I do care about who's my teacher and who is my advisor. So I was told that some of the [ranking] checklist or rubric that they use that gives the university [its] ranking, is the football team. ...I don't care about the football team. I do care about who's the person that gives me the knowledge. That's my biggest concern. (104)

6. The study also summarized that Saudis' decision to study abroad is influenced by family and cultural and religious factors, especially in the case of female participants.

Study 12

The Title of the study: SAUDI STUDENTS' EXPERIENCE OF INTERCULTURAL COMMUNICATION			
The Researcher name:	Suliman Al-Musaiteer	University	The University of Akron
Year of study:	2015	Type of research	Thesis, Master of Arts in Education
Research methodology	Qualitative	The Instruments for data collection	Semi-structured interview

Number of participants	3 male students		

Chosen Direct Quotations

- In the light of the research questions about how Saudi students experienced intercultural communication in the USA, what factors encouraged and discouraged them when seeking to initiate communication with Americans, I found that the Saudi students' perceptions about intercultural communication were positive in general. They understood the importance of the intercultural communication. They saw its impact on developing their life and language skills. It also improved their academic achievement and helped them to acquire the cultural knowledge of the host culture. (p. 76)

- In general, I was surprised about the positivity of my participants' experience. I thought their experience with communicating with Americans would be more negative and that they would discuss the barriers rather than the motivators The reason behind this perception is the literature that I found, which mainly indicated the difficulties and challenges, rarely mentioning the success (Gareis, 2012; Harrison, 2011; HinchcliffPelias & Greer, 2004; Lin & Rancer, 2003; Neuliep & Ryan, 1998; Yue & Lê, 2013). (p. 76)

- The mutual interest might be sports, shared similar values, or smoking hookah, according to the participants. For example, Bader noticed that his friend in the lab was a devoted Christian, so when he talked about religion, he found that his friend was interested in this topic even though their religions were different. Ali, for instance, came from a country that is not famous for playing basketball or football, but when he saw that Americans liked playing these sports, he tried to be good at them, and this helped him to become more involved with Americans. (p. 78)

- All of the participants reported that they communicated with American people to increase their cultural awareness of American culture, although Ali and Bader were interested in learning more about American culture before they came to the U.S. since they were fond of it, while Ahmed was not interested in American culture until after he came to the U.S. In spite of the different interests, all of the participants agreed that knowing American culture would facilitate their life in the U.S. and let them engage more fully with members of the local American community. (p. 80)

Significant findings

1. The Saudi students were more willing to interact with American people when they benefited from their classmates academically, such as when they got help with understanding course materials or got their notes.

2. Communicating with Americans helped the Saudis improve their English skills and learn the American accent. Also, interactions with Americans helped the Saudis understand American culture better.

3. The participants believed that Americans are interested in communicating with Saudi students who are skillful in sports or perform well in a class because this shows how smart and exciting the students are.

4. Talking about sports and religious matters may be a reason to start friendly relations between Saudi and local students. Saudi students were more motivated to communicate with Americans who respected their culture and religion.

5. Saudis were disinclined to be involved in intercultural talks when they felt that their integrity was threatened. Furthermore, Saudi students felt intimidated when their contact with Americans distracted them from their priorities and goals. Also, the findings showed that the negative stereotypes of

both Saudi and American people blocked the interactions between the Saudis and the nationals.

Study 13

The Title of the study: **Saudi Student Integration in Southeastern U.S. Institutions: A Study on the Impact of Academic, Social, and Cultural Adjustments Related to Academic Success**			
The Researcher name:	Carrie Marie Melius	University	Auburn University
Year of study:	2017	Type of research	dissertation
Research methodology	mixed methods,		

Chosen Direct Quotations

> Another aspect that surfaced from the participant responses was the experience of being befriended by domestic students only to have students attempt to proselytize them. These scenarios usually began with domestic students initiating friendships with participants and making it appear to genuinely be interested in them, but then later students discovered that the attempts for friendships by domestic students were followed by invitations to church or discussions regarding religion. (p. 109)

> Most students felt excitement before arriving in the United States because they were coming to a new place and culture as well as having a lot of advantages, "the peak of everything" as Willy put it. Some students expressed excitement pre-arrival because they thought the United States would be like the Hollywood film version because it was the only exposure they had to the culture of the United States. (p. 135)

Lack of learning critical thinking skills in the Saudi Arabian educational system was another area in which Saudi students felt created more challenges during their academic studies. Participants mentioned that instructors did not use a variety of teaching methods as found in the United States and that instruction in Saudi Arabia was mainly based on rote memorization of the subject material. (p.138)

Students also expressed that they were not taught study skills, such as note-taking and studying for tests, and that most of the instructors in Saudi Arabia gave students the exact information that would be on the test. Active learning from an individualistic perspective took some adjustment for participants who were used to being taught in a collective setting where there was less responsibility placed on the individual and more on the teacher's expertise and the students. (p. 139)

Significant findings

1. Two of the reasons why Saudi participants choose to study in the United States are the reputation and strength of its higher education system.

2. The participants found that Americans were typically friendlier than they had initially anticipated; however, Saudis shared that they found it more difficult to make authentic friendships with the Americans, after their arrival.

3. The lack of English preparation was one of the most significant academic challenges for participants in this research.

4. Many Saudi students felt that they were not adequately prepared by their Saudi schools in their command of the English language, which is required in the academic environment at U.S. universities.

5. Because the participants were less proficient in English before entering an academic program in the United States, one particular difficulty for them was the amount of academic reading that was required of them.

6. The majority of students reported that they sometimes came to class without completing their readings or assignments. while others never completed them.

7. The lack of critical thinking skills within the Saudi Arabian educational system was another challenging area for Saudi students during their academic studies in U.S. universities.

8. Most participants believed that their experience of, and relationship with, their instructors were positive. They also did not hesitate to ask questions and to visit the office of the professors to ask for help.

9. Feelings of depression, loneliness, and homesickness were common obstacles among Saudis in this study.

10. Participants reported having difficulty with American students' lack of understanding and misconceptions of their culture, which made adjusting to the host culture more challenging.

11. Many Saudi participants faced discrimination and negative perspectives from domestics on campus and off based on being from Saudi Arabia as well as their outer appearance.

12. The majority of participants did not feel that their cultural adjustment had any significant influence on their academic success.

13. Generally, participants believed in the required core courses, such as history and humanities, which were more complicated than the major courses.

14. Most participants benefited from academic support services on campus, both content-based and for English instruction.

15. The study found no statistical significance among demographic variables, including age, gender, credit hours per semester, year of study, and length of stay, with academic success or the total adjustment score.

16. Controlling the environment, communication/collaboration with others, self-motivation, and self-reflection were success strategies that Saudi students applied to overcome challenges and succeed.

Summary

The chapter presented a collection of studies conducted on Saudi international students in American higher education institutions throughout approximately half a century. This part of the book illustrates a number of common experiences and challenges that Saudi students encounter while studying and living in the United States, as cited in the literature. Many studies have found that government scholarship programs that fund Saudi learning in the United States and the excellent reputation of American universities around the world have been motivators and critical reasons for choosing to come to the United States to study.

The researchers found that a lack of English proficiency causes adjustment difficulties for Saudi students with the host culture. Further, language barriers are the primary academic challenge for Saudis in the U.S., especially in academic writing. At the same time, Saudis experience difficulties reading, taking notes, and participating in class discussions. Cultural shocks, loneliness, and homelessness are problems for Saudis, but these problems are reduced with time.

The marital status also shows frequently as a significant factor in several studies in this chapter, and the researchers discovered that single students faced more academic challenges than married students. Financial problems were cited in some studies among the difficulties encountered by Saudi students, but at the same time, the results indicate that the Saudis face less economic challenges compared to other international students in the United States because Saudis usually receive financial aid and scholarships from the Saudi government, which cover tuition and living expenses.

As indicated in these studies, Saudis found that Americans were typically friendlier than they had initially anticipated before they arrived in the United States; however, they found it a challenge to make authentic friendships with the Americans, after their arrival. Saudi students also faced varying degrees of discrimination while living in the United States. Generally, the findings of the above studies found that the Saudi's expectations of the United States that did not match reality; for example, they expected it to be an unsafe country where gangs and killings exist, just as they are portrayed in the Hollywood movies, and they also expected there to be intolerance and racism against Muslims. However, these expectations differed from reality, because they discovered that the American people were tolerant and friendly and that the United States is a secure country and not as it is presented in cinemas. Most Saudi students in this study had positive and satisfactory experiences while living and studying in the United States, and they had good relations with their professors.

Part two

Saudi students, as Arabs, have characteristics and patterns that distinguish them from the rest of the foreign students in the United States, especially Asians, whose issues and experiences at American institutions of higher education are of most interest to researchers. Although the number of Saudi students in the United States has rapidly increased in recent years, journal studies, books, and other publications on this group are still limited. Accordingly, I decided to attach a second part to this book that has some information on how Saudi students live in the United States and details of the daily life of Saudis that I met. It is good to state here that all information in this section is based on my observations and my perceptions of a large number of Saudi students, friends, and classmates, especially those in the language study stage. In the other section, I will briefly present my story as a Saudi international student in the United States. The purpose of sharing my story is to enrich the content on Saudi students in the United States and invite other Saudis who studied in the States to post their experiences and stories because the existing information is minimal. It is also worth knowing that three chapters of part two of this book were written before the chapters in the first part to guarantee that the information and knowledge from the studies on Saudi students in the United States do not influence the topics of this part.

Chapter Five: The way of life of Saudis in the USA

This chapter covers various subjects related to the way of life of students coming from Saudi Arabia who study at language institutions (ESL) and colleges of the United States. I attempt to choose the most significant points about the Saudis in the United States. Some of the topics may seem a bit unfamiliar, but these topics are essential for documenting a specific and exceptional period that witnessed an incredible increase of Saudis in the States. In this section, I will try as much as possible to be objective and convey my perceptions on the lives of Saudi students in the States apart from my personal experience, which I will address in the next part of this book.

Saudis and their children

A large number of Saudi students bring their families and children with them during their studies in the United States, and the Saudi government facilities that by paying a monthly salary for all the students who have scholarships and their families who move to the United States, and students who have more kids with receive more money from the government compared to students who do not have children. The Saudi government does not only give monthly allowances to the students and their families but also urges the students and their families to learn; the government will pay all the tuition fees for Saudis in the USA. As a result, in most cases, all the members of the family will become students when they arrive in the USA and study in ESL schools or in colleges.

However, Saudis who have children will face difficulties since the person who has the scholarship and his/her spouse are both students and spend long hours each day in college. As a result, Saudi parents in the USA usually cannot take care of their children all day because these parents are full-time students. Consequently, the students who have children find it difficult to find a suitable place to put their children while they are in college.

One of the favorite places for Saudis to send their children is in nurseries or daycares. Most Saudi students face two significant difficulties with daycares; the first problem is daycares are often expensive for them, and these places charge a lot of money especially because the Saudis have high fertility and have big families. The biggest problem is the lack of the number of nurseries or daycare, especially daycares near universities campuses, which lead many Saudis to register their kids with waiting lists for these caring centers and to hire a baby sitter to take care of their children in their homes while waiting for an available place for their kids in daycare centers.

Saudi students who have school-aged children have better educational options compared to Saudis who have infants or toddlers. Saudis can send their children to the public schools in the neighborhood that they live for free tuition, and some schools provide transportation services for these kids. Some Saudis who live in major cities may prefer to send their children to private Islamic schools because this kind of school teaches Islamic and Arabic courses. Accordingly, these young Saudi students in Islamic schools in the United States will not face a major cultural shock after returning to study in Saudi schools when their parents finish their studies at American universities.

Places of Prayer

As Muslims, Saudis are required to pray five times a day and night. Prayers in Islam are different from prayers in Christianity. Prayers in Islam have specific times with start and end periods. For instance, the Maghrib prayer, which is the fourth prayer of the day, begins at sunset and ends approximately one and a half hours later. Saudi students do not have difficulty finding places of prayer and worship outside of school because most cities—even small ones—have mosques or Islamic centers. In some big cities, several mosques perform the five prayers. However, many Saudi students find it difficult to perform some prayers when they are in university settings since not all institutions have dedicated places for prayers.

When I was a student at the Language Institute in Pullman, the Saudi students could not find a decent area on campus where they could perform the noon prayer. Saudis also could not go to the mosque that is 10 minutes away from the institute by car or half an hour on foot because students had only a 50-minute break for lunch, and the time for the Dhuhr prayer begins during the last 10 minutes of this break. Therefore, the students had to find a place inside the institute to pray. Some students prayed in empty classrooms during the break, while others prayed in the computer lab. Fortunately, with an increase in the number of Saudis and a few students from Omani and Kuwait at the Language Institute in Pullman, the administration of the institute decided to allocate a special room on the fourth floor of the same school building. The place was called the quiet room, and they put a rug in it. Then they announced that all students who wanted to practice their religious rituals should go to that room.

With the opening of the room, many Saudi and Arab students felt good in the Institute, before, the quiet room was not accessible to these students, to find a suitable place to perform Aduher prayer and sometimes Asr prayer, because students spent most of their day in the ESL schools from 8 am till 4 pm, four days a week. And during this time, at least one prayer time begins and ends during school time. On Friday, the study time of ESL schools starts from 8 am until 12:30 pm, so Muslim students have time to go to the mosque to attend Jumu'ah or called Friday Prayer.

Saudis and exercise

I noticed that many Saudi students in the United States agree that their health practices improved after coming to America. I have heard many students talking about increasing their physical activity in the United States. I also saw many young Saudis riding bicycles, wandering around their campus and apartments, which is considered a new habit for the majority of Saudis because Saudis, in general, are less active and often use cars, even for short trips or shopping from stores located close to their homes.

Despite the fact that many pieces of literature showed that international Asian students are more likely to gain weight while studying in America due to the American fast food that has many calories, I have noticed many Saudis lost a significant amount of weight in the US. According to my Saudi friends who lost weight, the loss is due to two main reasons: The main reason is that these Saudis have become more active in America because they have to be independent. Saudi students have to do all the chores by themselves, such as doing laundry, cleaning the apartments, and vacuuming their homes. The second reason why these Saudis lost kilograms of weight was the nature of social life in America, where the majority of people had no time to cook food every day. Accordingly, the Saudis did not have the opportunity to eat traditional Saudi foods that had hundreds of calories. At the same time, there were no Saudi restaurants. I heard that Saudi students attended university gyms more regularly in America than they did in KSA. One possible reason why they attended gyms was so that they could meet their Saudi friends and play football and video games. Also, many male Saudi students wanted to build their bodies by lifting weights so that they would look good to female American students.

In addition, gyms clarify the differences between Saudi culture and American culture. Gyms in KSA are segregated based on gender. Accordingly, females have their own gyms, and males have their own gyms. On the other hand, gyms in the U.S. are for both genders. Thus, male Saudis were able to exercise and share the swimming pool with female students for the first time in their lives. Moreover, it was funny to hear new Saudi students talking about their reaction to seeing American males showering naked in gyms; while this was perceived as normal behavior in the U.S., it would have been shameful in KSA.

Saudis and Ramadan

Ramadan is the ninth month of the Islamic calendar, and the Islamic calendar is a lunar calendar just like the Jewish one. In Ramadan, all Muslims , except for some categories such as patients and travelers, fast from dawn to sunset. It is also vital to know that fasting in Islam is different from fasting in some Christian doctrines that refrain from eating some types of food. Fasting in the Islamic teachings requires Muslims to abstain from all drinks, foods, and sex activities throughout the fasting time. Due to the lunar Islamic calendar, the month of Ramadan moves among the seasons of the year every several years. In recent years the month of Ramadan has fallen in the summertime, which means that Muslims have to fast for longer hours, more than 17 hours a day.

Muslim Saudi students in the United States fast long hours at the same time they are studying in colleges, which may make their energies and attention not in normal states due to the lack of nutrients. Therefore, American teachers must take care of their Muslim students during the month of Ramadan. One example among many that show how American teachers can be supportive of their Muslim students during Ramadan is that I noticed a number of American teachers avoiding drinking water in front of their Saudi students. These teachers did not want to harm the feelings of their students, which is a noble act.

Saudis and friendships with the Americans

Many studies on foreign students in the US stated that foreign students believe that Americans are nice people, but at the same time these students think they face difficulties in making effective friends with the Americans. I agree with the results of these studies fully. During my observation I found it difficult to make friends with the Americans, except for the missionaries who are with foreign students intensively through student clubs and other social activities in campuses. The studies provided many causes that led to international students having difficulty building relationships with local students, such as cultural differences, and particularly language issues. Many non-native students have weak English-speaking abilities, which makes it harder for locals to have long conversations with these people.

I think one of the reasons it is difficult for Saudis to make friends with American students, along with poor language skills, is religious differences. Some Saudis Muslim students may avoid making friends with some Americans because many Saudis believe all Americans live the Hollywood way. In Hollywood movies, actors portray the majority of Americans as playboys who drink alcohol all day long. Accordingly, some conservative Saudi students worry that when making friendships with Americans, the Yankees will lead the Saudis to corruption and immorality.

On the other hand, the Saudis in general also avoid American students who work with missionary organizations, either Protestant or Jehovah's Witnesses, who are considered by most Christians to be outside Christianity. The main reason for these Saudis to avoid missionaries is that the Saudis are not used to discussions about religious differences, and the Saudis may fear that these missionaries will be able to change their religious convictions.

Saudis and SMOKING

A review of the statistics on the problem of smoking among Saudis in Saudi Arabia is essential to understand the issue of smoking among Saudi students in the United States. The statistics that will be presented include smoking all types of tobacco, including cigarettes and shisha or hookah, as it is called in the U.S. Smoking statistics in Saudi Arabia indicate a high rate of smoking significantly even though smoking is prohibited practices for Muslims because according to Islamic teachings harmful things are not permitted.

According to the Ministry of Health in Saudi Arabia (2014) "overall, 12.1% of Saudis reported that they currently smoke tobacco. This prevalence was 23.7%among males and 1.5% among females. The prevalence of tobacco smoking varied by age; among those aged 65 and older, the incidence of tobacco smoking was the lowest: 6.5% (9.7% among males and 1.8% among females). Saudis aged 55 to 64 years had the highest prevalence of current smoking

(15.6%) with 24.7% among males and 4.2% among females" (p. 1) Smoking is often confined to indoor homes, cafes or cars in the Middle East just as it was decades ago in the United States. Indoor smoking is particularly harmful to people who inhale smoke from non-smokers or (secondhand smoke and passive smoking). According to The Saudi Health Interview Survey (SHIS) (2014) "17.2% of Saudis are exposed to secondhand smoke at home, with an average of 5.1 days of exposure per week. This secondhand exposure is 20.9%, with an average of 4.8 days of exposure per week, for males, and 13.1%, with an average of 5.5 days of exposure per week, for females.14.8% of Saudis are exposed to secondhand smoke at work, with an average of 2.2 days of exposure per week. This secondhand exposure at work affects 24.9% of males, with an average of 4.3 days of exposure per week, and 2.6% of females, with an average of 1.4 days of exposure per week". (p. 2)

As you noted in the previous statistics on smoking in Saudi Arabia, the number of Saudi smokers is large, and when they come to the United States to study, they retain the habit of smoking, unfortunately. There were many stories about Saudi students smoking at the ESL school where I studied in Washington State, and I am sure that similar situations have arisen in many other ESL schools around the U.S. due to the large number of Saudi students who were studying English between 2008 and 2016.One of the recurring stories involving new Saudi students was about smoking near entrances and school doors even though American law restricts smokers to a specific distance from school gates and public places. Accordingly, the administrators at the ESL institute repeatedly have to tell Saudi smokers not to vaporize near the entrance because the state law requires smokers to keep away from entrances at a distance of approximately 20 feet. I noticed that smoking is only popular among male Saudi students, and I have not seen more than 10 Saudi women who smoke. I have also noted that smoking is popular among male Asian ESL students, especially Chinese students. The Chinese male students smoked heavily several times during the school day, showing a strong preference for cigarettes manufactured in China, while, at the same time, I did not notice any such behavior from the Korean or Japanese students except on rare occasions.

A negative thing I observed was that many of the young Saudi students did not become smokers until after arriving in the United States. I believe the reason is that these Saudis, who are often under the age of 20, are free, for the first time in their lives, from parental control and, perhaps, are also new to knowing or having smokers in their lives. One of the most important things that initially grabbed the attention of these Saudi smokers was the strict rules they encountered when they went to buy cigarettes from convenience stores. For example, the law says that those who want to buy cigarettes must show their ID cards and be over the age of 18. This was a challenge for many Saudis during their first days in the U.S. because they did not have personal identification cards. Furthermore, some cashiers still asked Saudis aged over 30 to show their ID cards, so it is no surprise that many Saudis expressed their displeasure at the rules around cigarettes in this new environment. Also, one of the hot topics among Saudi smokers is cigarette prices, since cigarette prices fluctuate between states. For instance, the price of a pack of cigarettes in Pullman was almost $10 in 2013, while the price of the same cigarette brand in Moscow, Idaho, which is only 10 minutes away, does not exceed $5 for a pack.

Saudi students who smoke are heavy smokers in general and prefer to smoke during break times between classes. Saudi students prefer American cigarettes such as Marlboro, which are prevalent in Saudi Arabia, but at the same time, some Saudis believe that the flavor of cigarettes in America is better than those in Saudi Arabia. Cigarettes in Saudi Arabia are of higher quality, although cigarettes carry the same brand and models.

Aside from the high proportion of Saudi smokers of cigarettes, there is a large proportion of Saudis who prefer smoking shisha or, as the Americans call it, hookah. Hookah is explained by Oxford Dictionary (2010) as " a kind of tobacco pipe in which the smoke is drawn through water to cool it" (p. 386). Shisha smoking is generally considered to be socially acceptable behavior in Arab societies. However, smoking for young people and adolescents in the same place where their parents or uncles sit is mostly unacceptable. Smoking shisha is a favorite in all Arabic countries and many Middle Eastern regions. In Saudi Arabia, many cafes offer shisha to consumers, and there are numerous cafes specializing in the hookah.

Many Saudi international students bring tobacco and their shisha, which is often manufactured in Egypt when they move from the KSA to the United States to study. Saudis also easily find many smoking stores offering hookah, and most of them smoke the double apple tobacco flavor. Frequently, Saudis smoke hookah every day at night time, and they spend about an hour or more smoking to adjust their mood, as they usually describe.

When I was in Pullman and Seattle in WA, I noticed that the number of cafes or special bars offering shisha increased very fast. For example, in 2013, only four hookah bars were opened in the city of Seattle. and I heard that the number jumped in the last few years. One of the reasons for the rise in the number of shisha cafes or bars is the presence of Saudis, who are considered the biggest customers of shisha cafes. One of the new things that I observed in shisha cafes in America was that a number of people shared the same shisha. I often saw three or sometimes four friends sharing the same hookah hose, which is not common in Arab countries, where everyone smokes from his own hookah.

Saudis and Cars

Most male Saudi students buy used cars within a few weeks of their arrival in the United States. These young students are often cheated by car dealership owners because students do not have the ability to distinguish good cars from poor cars. In general, used car prices in America are often reasonable and cheaper than those in the KSA. However, the big difficulty for Saudis in the US is not buying cars but maintaining those cars and making them run. Car maintenance is too expensive in the United States compared to the KSA due to high labor costs. Furthermore, Saudis usually do not have the mechanical skills to maintain their cars, unlike Americans. Many Americans do their own maintenance, so they can save a lot of money. On the other hand, Saudis usually head directly to maintenance shops when they have a problem with their cars because it's not too expensive to repair their cars in the KSA. Accordingly, many Saudi students in the US are leaving their cars idle for several days and perhaps weeks until they receive salaries from the Saudi government, and some of the students owe money because they borrow it from their friends to repair their cars.

Rising and rapidly changing gasoline prices are also a reason for the Saudi students' budgets, because gasoline prices in America are much higher than in Saudi Arabia. Interestingly, one of the new situations for the Saudis who own cars in America is gasoline stations in America. In most US states, gasoline stations are self-service, since the owner of the car is the one who fills the gasoline in the car by using credit cards. In Saudi Arabia, there are workers serving at the petrol stations. Car owners sit inside the vehicle during the filling of fuel, and then the driver of the car gives cash to the gas station worker directly. Regulations in most US states give Saudi students the opportunity to drive cars for the first year after their arrival using Saudi driving licenses, but insurance companies raise their prices to insure vehicles driven by persons holding foreign driver's licenses. After one obtains a driver's license from a US state, insurance rates on vehicles are significantly reduced and prices become reasonable.

Saudi female students and driving cars in the USA

Many Saudi women who study abroad, including in the US, experienced a new thing for them, which was driving cars. The issue of banning women from driving in the KSA was a hot topic for Saudi society and foreign media. Also, the issue of women driving was used as political pressure against the KSA for decades. Luckily, in 2018, Saudi women officially got the right to drive in the KSA, which ended this controversial issue in Saudi society.

During my time living in the States, I saw many male Saudi friends trying to teach their daughters, sisters, or wives how to drive. It was also a good experience to see Saudi females driving and get their licenses. At the same time, the majority of female Saudi students did not drive cars by 2018. I expect that more female Saudi students who will study in the US in the coming years will drive here because they will learn to drive in their home country.

Saudis and food culture shock

American food is not new for the majority of Saudis. Saudis generally are fans of modern American food, and American restaurants are spread throughout Saudi cities, even in some villages and rural areas. Many of the most famous restaurants in the US are in Saudi Arabia, such as McDonald's, Hardee's, Burger King, KFC, Domino's Pizza, and Pizza Hut. Further, what is called "neighborhood restaurant" like Applebee's and Fridays are well-known to the Saudis, and people wait for a long time to find a table to dine there.I think the reasons that led to the spread of American food and American restaurants in Saudi Arabia and the world, in general, are Hollywood movies and the fact that American food is tasty and quick to prepare. However, many physicians and educators blame American food and drinks like colas as well as American restaurants for the many health problems among the Saudis especially the youth. According to the Ministry of Health, in 2017, about 40% of Saudi citizens were classified as overweight or obese, and about 20% of Saudis had diabetes.

The Saudis miss Saudi food and restaurants when they are in the United States. Arab and Middle Eastern restaurants are widespread in large cities, but they do not serve Saudi food, which differs significantly from the Lebanese and Turkish cuisines. Indian restaurants are the best options for Saudis because modern Saudi food in the last two centuries has been inspired by Indian cooking. For example, one of the traditional Saudi foods is Al-Kabsa, which is made from rice imported from India, Indian spices, and pieces of meat. Many of my American friends have told me they do not find a vast difference between Indian food and Al-Kabsa, except that Indians put more spices in their food. I agree with these Americans. Al-Kabsa was not originally what Arabs ate in the past; authentic Arab food is made of dates, meat, wheat, milk, honey, and corn, in the southern regions.

Saudis and Arab grocery markets

Saudi Arabian international students usually bring with them some food, Arabic coffee, spices, and serving utensils, including Arabic coffee and teacups from their country because these things are not available in most regions in the United States. Also, Saudis are loyal customers of Arabic grocery stores. In recent years, as Arab and Muslim populations have doubled in the United States, Arab groceries that provide Arab food have been opened in many large US cities. Arabic markets and restaurants are usually more expensive when compared to normal stores; however, Saudis like to go to Arabic stores because they usually stock items preferred by Saudis.

The most common items that Saudis buy from Arab grocery stores and are not available in supermarkets such as Wal-Mart are Halal meat and chicken, Arabic spices, Egyptian beans, Arabic bread, cheese, tea, and dates. Many Arabic stores provide shipping services, so you can order dry food like Arabic coffee and dates via the internet and get it within two days. Amazon has also started to compete with Arabic food stores, and it sells Arabic foods and sweets at reasonable prices.

Saudis and Time

American teachers commonly complain about the attendance of their Saudi students and say these students do not respect time. The professors and teachers complain that Saudi students come to class late and do not submit their homework on time. Therefore, it is important to explain that one of the major differences between Arabic and American cultures is the concept of time. Americans, in general, are well organized in their lives and respect time very much and say time is money. One example among many that shows how the Americans value time is dining time; all American students and employees have their lunch between noon and 1 p.m., and the majority of American families eat their dinner at 6 p.m. On the other hand, the majority of Arabs do not value time, and their dining times explain this issue. For example, there is no specific time for lunch or dinner; even I have my dinner and lunch at different times. Accordingly, Americans who deal with Arabs need to understand that if Arab students come late, that does not mean they are shameless; it is just part of their culture.

Saudis and Communicating with Their Family in KSA

Saudi students in American colleges in the 80s and 90s had only two options to communicate with their families: by telephone, which were very costly for these students, or by writing letters that took about two months to arrive. I clearly remember when I was young, my mom read a letter from her brother who was studying in Florida. He attached in his letter a picture of his newborn boy. Also, some wealthy students used fax to communicate with their friends and parents.

Fortunately, the internet revolution led to the creation of many telecommunications applications, such as

Skype, WhatsApp, and IMO. These apps have helped Saudi international students to communicate with their relatives face to face easily and freely via using the internet, and in real time. Furthermore, social media networks such as Facebook, Twitter, and Instagram, among others, allow Saudi students to chat with friends in KSA directly without caring about the cost for phone provider companies like in the past. The internet also helped Saudi students in America to read Arabic publications daily and to learn about political, economic, and sports news back home. The developments in communication technology have also allowed Saudi students in the United States to watch Arab TV channels. Watching TV is essential for Saudis, especially since male Saudis want to follow Saudi sports championships, especially in soccer, and are loyal to their teams even while studying outside of their country.

Saudis and English

English is the main academic obstacle for Saudi students studying in the United States, and it is an obstacle for students of other nationalities as well. Most Saudis spend several months in the United States studying English at language institutes that teach English as a second language to improve their language skills and help them score high in the TOEFL and IELTS tests. After scoring high in TOEFL or IELTS, Saudis get academic admission to start their higher education journey in the United States. The main reason for the weakness of the English skills of Saudis is due to the ineffective English methods in the general Saudi schools compared to the teaching of English language to other countries such as India and South Korea. For example, Indian students are directly accepted by US universities because their TOEFL scores are high; Indian schools have clear goals in making Indian students proficient in English language skills

Saudis and churches

According to official statistics in Saudi Arabia, all Saudis follow the Islamic religion. As is known, Saudi Arabia is an Islamic state and not a secular one, so the government supports the building and maintenance of mosques. When you visit Saudi Arabia, you will find that mosques are scattered everywhere. Informal statistics indicate that the number of mosques in Saudi Arabia is about 100,000 places of worship for Muslims in KSA. Given that the Saudis are all Muslims, in addition, the most sacred civilizations of the Muslims are Mecca and Medina, which are located in Saudi Arabia. There are no public places of worship for non-Muslims yet, such as churches, synagogues, and those for other religions. Accordingly, Saudi Arabian international students in the U.S. will experience a culture shock when they see churches and synagogues for the first time in their lives, especially because many Saudi students have not left Saudi Arabia before coming to America.

I also noted that Saudis advise each other to stay away from American missionaries who are trying to help foreign students develop their English language skills by talking to them and correcting their speaking mistakes, as well as helping these students with pronunciation for free. Moreover, the missionaries, most of whom are college students, organize many activities for international students on weekends and holidays, such as bowling, watching NFL games, and hiking. The main reason why Saudis advise each other to avoid making friends with missionaries is that the ultimate aim of missionaries is to convert foreign students to Christianity. In collective societies, such as the

Arab one, changing religion is a difficult decision that carries many consequences and risks for the individual and his family.

Saudis and studying in mixed classes

Saudi public and private schools and colleges are single-sex education centers where Saudi males and females study separately. Therefore, Saudis will experience a cultural shock in their first weeks of studying in the US. For the first time in their lives, Saudis will have classmates of the opposite gender. I have heard many stories from my male Saudi friends, narrating their experiences of studying with females for the first time. They did not feel comfortable because female students were smart and hardworking learners. Further, Saudi male students also have opposite sex teachers because most ESL teachers are women. According to many male Saudi students, female teachers are gentler and more patient than male teachers, especially in teaching learners who speak English as a second language, which requires teachers to be calm and patient.

Summary

This chapter attempted to give readers a quick overview of some of the subjects related to the Saudi people living in the United States for studying. Saudi students usually face a lot of cultural problems in the first months in the States, and then things get better for them as they adapt to the culture of the host country. In the next part, I will briefly inform you about my personal experiences in the United States. This next part is divided into two chapters. The first chapter presents my first two-years in the States, where I was studying at two ESL schools. The final section of this book contains topics related to my experience in American universities.

Chapter Six: My story in the United States, the first two years

Chapter Six: My story in the United States, the first two years

There are vast differences between the way of life and culture in Saudi Arabia and America; accordingly, I want to share some of the details and attitudes I encountered in the United States in the first months of my arrival to the dreamland. This chapter briefly presents my last days in Saudi Arabia before coming to the United States, including the way I received a visa from the Embassy of Washington in Riyadh. The chapter also presents the various significant events and daily details that I had after my arrival in Washington, D.C. and my first day there, where I had difficulty due to the lack of my English proficiency. This section also summarizes the most important details of the first two years of my life as a foreign student in the United States at ESL institutes because my language skills at that time did not qualify me to join a university directly. The chapter is generally divided into three sections. The first part shows my last days in Saudi Arabia and my early days in the US capital, and the second piece summarizes my story in the small town of Pullman where I spent nearly a full year at a language institute. The last part of this chapter covers my most remarkable experiences in my second year in the United States, where I moved to Seattle, WA.

After serving for a few months as a teacher at an elementary public school in a city 250 miles northeast of Riyadh, I received a proposal to work as a teacher assistant at the same college where I received my bachelor's degree. Accordingly, I decided to leave my job as a classroom teacher in a public school and go and work in the higher education sector. The main reason to accept the new position was that working in higher education offers teacher assistants the opportunity to continue post-graduate education. After changing my career and working as a teacher at the College of Education, King Saud University in Riyadh, the capital of Saudi Arabia, I was inspired by many of the officials and my former professors to study abroad, especially in the United States, which has the best system of higher education in the world. At the same time, the university administration provided me with a full scholarship to study English, then a master's, and then a doctorate in the United States, and the deal was a very attractive offer for me and could not be rejected.

Once I received a full external academic scholarship from King Saud University to study in the United States, I started asking people who had already graduated from American universities about my next step to know the best place and ESL school for me. Among those people was my former professor, Dr. Abdul Aziz al-Muqail, who received his doctorate from the University of Idaho in Moscow a few years before I moved to the United States to study English. Dr. Al-Maqqil suggested that I travel to a city called Pullman, Washington, located close to the town of Moscow because Pullman is a safe city and has cheap home rentals compared to large cities. He added that when I get accepted by the ESL school in Pullman, which belongs to Washington State University (WSA), and I would get a conditional admission to be a master's student at this university upon completing all the levels at the ESL school. I followed Dr. Aziz al-Maqil's advice, and I decided to study in Pullman, Washington. Accordingly, I went to an agency that deals with international universities and institutes and brings admissions to Saudis who plan to study abroad. I told the agency to contact the Intensive American Language Center (IALC), which is run by WSU, and get an admission form from it. After a few weeks, the agency reached the agency and informed me that it had received the admission form, I-20, from the institute, which was one of the requirements to get a full-time student visa, or an F1 visa, from the US Embassy.

After receiving full documentation from the Language Institute in Pullman, I have started procedures to get a visa from the embassy in Riyadh so that I can travel to the U.S. and begin my education journey there. Going to the US embassy is different from the rest of the embassies in Saudi Arabia. Most embassies do not require prior scheduling appointments. However, the situation is different for the US Embassy, which requires booking an appointment via the website. The US Embassy's website asks a lot of documents to get an interview with employees of the embassy. I remember facing difficulty with this website, and it took a few days to complete all the website requirements. After completing all the steps in the embassy's electronic webpage, the site showed me some available times to meet the embassy officials, and the earliest opportunity to meet was after a full month. After choosing the day of the interview with officials of the US Embassy in Riyadh, I searched on Google about what the US Embassy staff commonly ask Saudis who plan to study or visit the USA. I found tens interesting stories about that; however, I believed that the general impression of the embassy staff was negative at that time. For example, there have been many complaints that the embassy staff purposely provoke Saudis by asking them about their relationship with terrorism or extremist groups. I have also read stories about the embassy staff's lack of respect for Saudis, as well as to the other visitors to the embassy. During that time, in the summer of 2011, some friends also recommended that I stay calm and be ready for any question from the embassy officials.

On the day of the interview, I went to the embassy early. If I remember correctly, the meeting was at 9:45 am. The inspection procedures were intensive and precise, and there were security men armed with machine guns everywhere inside and outside the embassy, which was an unfamiliar scene for me. After entering the building of the US embassy in Riyadh, I was astonished by the number of visitors. I believe there were more than 1,000 people waiting in seats for their turn to be interviewed by embassy staff; most of them were young Saudis who planned to study in the land of dreams. The embassy building in Riyadh was huge, lovely, air-conditioned and had a lot of comfortable chairs. A large number of employees worked for the U.S. embassy, many of them of Arab origin, because many of the visitors to the embassy were not fluent in English, just like me, at the time. My experience with the U.S. Embassy in Riyadh was fantastic, and I noticed that the staff treated people nicely. Moreover, I think the terrible stories about the embassy that I read online were not Accurate. After waiting for two hours, I heard someone calling my name in Arabic, "Saud Albeshr, go to window number 6." I went to the window, and there was a glass wall between the employee and me, just like the banks, to protect American employees in case a terrorist act happens. The female employee was an Asian-American woman; I saw her through the thick glass, and we communicated by phone, like what dangerous prisoners do with their visitors in Hollywood movies. The female employee spoke Arabic, not fluently but in an understandable way. She asked me questions and took some documents, such as my passport, diplomas, financial guarantees, and photographs. The conversation lasted only five minutes. She then told me that my papers were good, and they would give me a student visa within a few days through a post office that the embassy deals with.

Within five days, I received a call from the post office, stating that my passport was available with the U.S. visa inside it.

After getting my visa from the American Embassy in Riyadh, I started to prepare myself to travel to America. One of the biggest mistakes I made at that time was that I did not try seriously to learn English. Even though I had a lot of free time when I was in Riyadh, I thought I would learn English easily and quickly within a few months of arriving in the United States. Another mistake I have made was that I did not read or question about American culture, although many relatives and friends have studied there or visited the United States for tourism. Anyway, I went to the government travel office in Riyadh to get a free ticket to America. The flight itinerary was Riyadh, Washington DC, Seattle, then Pullman, WA. I planned to go to Washington DC first because I wanted to open an account in the Saudi Arabian Cultural Mission in the US (SACM). SACM represents the Saudi Ministry of Education in America, and their address had moved from DC to Virginia, which is less than 15 minutes away from the capital. I was a planner. After spending five days in the capital and completing all the procedures of SACM, I would move from Washington DC to Pullman, where there is a small airport that receives only three small planes a day from Seattle, as I believed. My trip to Washington, DC, was on Saudi Airlines on 30 September 2011. I could not come before that time because the U.S. authorities do not allow the holder of a student visa or F1 visa to enter American territory before 30 days of the first day of school shown on the Form 1-20 and the visa is valid for five years.

One of God's blessings is that I earned a full scholarship funded by the Saudi government to study abroad, and without it, I would not be able to explore the

States because I am from a family that is not rich and cannot afford to pay tuition and living expenses in America. The Saudi students who are receiving a scholarship funded by the Saudi government have several advantages such as:

- the Saudi government, through its representative, SACM, pays full tuition fees to American institutes and universities directly.
- Scholarship students receive free health insurance.
- The student gets a monthly salary from the Saudi government, approximately $1,840 and the pay is increasing as the number of family members increases. For example, a married student gets more than $3,000 per month, and if he or she has children, she will be given more money.
- Free annual travel tickets from U.S. cities to Saudi Arabia and many other services.

The travel day to America

I arrived at Riyadh International Airport five hours before the flight from Riyadh, KSA, to Washington, DC, departed. I went to the airport early based on the recommendation of US embassy officials, who told me that the procedures to travel to America take longer at the airport. For example, the inspections at airports for passengers from Riyadh to Washington are accurate, and the passengers are required to pass several checkpoints inside the airport to make sure they do not carry any prohibited materials with them onto the plane. I think the security procedures were more severe for passengers to America than they were for passengers to Asia and Europe due to strict security requirements from the US authorities at that time.

After a strict inspection procedure, we entered the aircraft, which took off at 3 am from Riyadh and then went to Jeddah, west of Saudi Arabia, where the plane stopped for 40 minutes. More passengers joined the plane from the Jeddah airport, which is about an hour away from Riyadh by flight. I did not know we would stop in Jeddah, but that was not a big deal. Even though we got more passengers from Jeddah, many, many seats on the plane were empty, so I used three chairs to make myself more comfortable on this long trip. It took 13 hours to reach Dulles International Airport

I arrived at Dulles Airport at 5 p.m., as far as I can remember, on September 30, 2011, after a long flight from Saudi Arabia. As soon as I entered the airport, I was transferred to the intensive inspection room by the security authorities. I expected this thing because I am a Saudi, Arabic and Muslim man, and many Saudis who visit the USA for the first time are more likely to face intensive inspection. Unfortunately, inspection procedures are still much tougher and longer with Saudis at US airports since the 9/11 attacks, and I have heard many stories about the suffering of Saudi people at US airports and their unfair treatment by some employees. I spent about four hours in the intensive room, and during that time, I was sitting in a chair, and nobody asked me anything. However, an Arabic passenger, who traveled from Riyadh with his small family, was annoyed by the long waiting time in the inspection room; accordingly, he went and complained to the officer. The passenger said he had a child and a wife who were tired of traveling, and he asked the officer kindly if they could finish the inspection as soon as possible so they could get out of the airport. However, the officer was angry with the Arabic passenger and said loudly, "Sit down, or I will take you back to your country."

After about four hours of waiting, the officer called my name and gave me my passport and two bags, which were subjected to intensive inspection according to the papers placed inside the bags. Then, the officer told me that I could now leave the airport. When I went out to the airport lounge, I saw staff from SACM. At the time, SACM had not changed its system or rolled out the new electronic system, and SACM employees received students from Saudi Arabia at Virginia Airport and then took them by bus to three-star hotels close to their new building. I ended up that night in a king-size room of a Sheraton hotel 15 minutes away from the airport, and I paid 80 dollars for each night.

Washington DC

After arriving in the United States on Friday, September 30, 2011, almost two weeks before I started my studies, I spent about five nights in the US capital and the state of Virginia, where the Saudi Arabian Cultural Mission to the US (SACM) is located. Because of my weekend arrival, I could not go to SACM in my first two days in the land of dreams. On Saturday, I woke up early and was surprised that the hotel lobby was full of dozens of Saudi students, both females and males, with few kids, and other hotels next to my hotel also had tons of new Saudi students. The SACM administration had made a deal with some hotels to host the new Saudi students for special rates for students. For example, the normal accommodation price in Sheraton Reston, VA, was $150 per night while a Saudi student could take a room for $80, or two Saudi students could share a two-bedroom for $40 per guest. Also, there were some Arabs in the lobby who offered their services to new Saudi students for large amounts of money and took advantage of these Saudis who did not have English abilities. They offered the following services:

- Help students open a bank account.
- Selling electrical plugs and outlets because they are different in Saudi Arabia than in the US.
- Giving a ride to Arabic restaurants.
- Sell U.S. SIM cards so the students can have an American phone number to make it cheaper and easier to communicate with people inside the U.S.
- The Arabs also offer to take the Saudis on tour to discover the attractions of Washington DC.

    I already planned that I would spend a full Saturday in Washington DC to visit the tourist attractions, and I asked the hotel staff how to go by bus to DC. He explained to me the way, which was taking the hotel shuttle to Reston downtown then take a bus, then I need to make the subway to reach Washington DC near the attractions, as far as I remember. Although my English was limited, I can explain what I want by showing the pictures and maps of the places that I want to visit. As planned, I went to the capital and visited the White House area, Capitol building, monuments, and beautiful museums which attracted me a lot. Accordingly, I have visited the Capital three times while living in the States, and I considered DC as my favorite city in America because of the existence of museums. The last trip to DC was in August 2018. My cousin and I visited the National Museum of African American History and Culture, which was opened by President Obama.

    On Sunday, I called a Saudi friend who was a student at one of the English institutes in Baltimore, so he took me from the Sheraton Hotel to Tysons Corner Center, which is one of the biggest shopping centers in the US, in his old sports car in the afternoon. At the center, I purchased a SIM card from T-Mobile based on my friend's recommendation. Then, we went to have lunch at TGI Friday's. I learned one thing about American culture during my lunch from my friend: customers in restaurants are expected to pay tips. I, like other Saudis, did not like tips much since we already paid a lot of money for our meals. It is important to explain that American restaurants and meals are very popular in all regions and cities of Saudi Arabia. In every neighborhood, there is almost every American restaurant, especially McDonald's, so American food is not new to Saudi students.

On Monday morning, I took a taxi with three Saudi students who were residing at the same hotel to SACM, and each person paid ten dollars for the taxi driver after their arrival at the modern SACM building in Fairfax, VA. There were a lot of new Saudi students who wanted to open an account in SACM, and SACM representatives of the Saudi Ministry of Higher Education in America. Accordingly, the staff of SACM is responsible for all Saudi students, so they pay salaries to students and pays tuition to colleges and schools. There were hundreds of new Saudi students in SACM; it was hard to talk with employees there due to the crowd. It is also important to understand, that even Saudi students in the U.S. who do not have a scholarship from the Saudi government, open accounts in SACM, so they can apply to get the scholarship while studying in the U.S. The majority of Saudi students gained their governmental scholarships while studying in the USA. Until 2015, thousands of Saudis came to study in America at their own expense, then opened an account in SACM and applied for governmental scholarships, and usually, they will get a full scholarship within a few weeks. I created an account at SACM that day, and I also realized that I could open the account from any place in America because SACM that time developed a useful virtual site and a smart application that provides a lot of services for Saudis such opening accounts and communicating with academic supervisors.

On Wednesday, I left the hotel and headed to Virginia Airport via the hotel shuttle. From there, I went to Seattle Airport and then to Pullman Regional Airport. My trip from Virginia to Seattle was by United Airlines, but the plane was old, and there was no screen for each seat like what modern airplanes have. The trip lasted about five hours, during which I felt hungry, so I asked a cabin crew if they had food. She said that they did not offer free food and that the passengers need to pay for the meals. I had no choice; I had to buy a meal because I was hungry. My Saudi Mastercard, however, did not work inside the plane, and I still do not know the reason because I have used it many times before and after this event. Fortunately, the cabin crew was nice and gave me the meal for free. This changed my impression of United Airlines from negative to positive.

Pullman

I arrived at Seattle airport, called Seattle-Tacoma International, from D.C. As I stated earlier, there was no direct flight from Washington, D.C. to Pullman; I had two options to reach Pullman, which was my final destination on this trip. The first option was going from D.C. to the airport in Spokane, WA, which is about 75 miles away from Pullman, so I would have to take a taxi or bus to Pullman. The second option was getting to Pullman directly from Seattle airport because the Pullman-Moscow Regional Airport is only several miles away from the hotel that I'd booked. The hotel was Super 8 Moscow in the state of Idaho, the state famous for potato production. The distance between Pullman, WA and Moscow, ID is only eight miles or approximately ten minutes by car.

Alaska Airlines' flight attendants called us to enter the jet on time to leave Seattle for Pullman, and I believed it was 11 p.m. The plane was tiny, the seats were narrow, and the engines sounded annoying, but the flight was only one hour, so it was tolerable to wait. However, something was not right in the air. There were heavy rain and thick fog in the Pullman area, so the pilot could not get off at Pullman airport despite his many attempts. After nearly two hours of trying, the pilot had to go to another nearby airport, which was Lewiston-Nez Perce County Regional Airport, about 40 miles from Pullman.

When we got off the small plane, thinking there were about 80 passengers, we found that the airport was dark and there were only five workers cleaning the airport because it was almost 2 a.m., and there were no flights at that time. The flight attendants of Alaska told us they would contact taxi companies in this city and neighboring cities to take us directly to our homes. However, in these small cities, there were not many taxis, so I had to wait for about three hours at the airport because the priority was families with children and older people, who got to go home first. After a long wait, I shared a taxi with four other passengers to Moscow, where I had rented a hotel for a week. Sadly, I could not bring my two big bags in the cab because there was not enough room for them. I thought I would lose the bags forever, but the Alaska employees brought them to the hotel where I was staying after only three hours.

On the afternoon of the first day, I took a taxi from the hotel where I was staying to the apartment rental agency in Pullman, Washington. I already knew of this office before

I came to Pullman; I had an agreement with them to rent a one-bedroom apartment, and I had paid the deposit a few weeks before arriving in Pullman. I did not know of many Saudis signing residential contracts before their arrival in America. However, I believed I was lucky to have signed the contract and gotten the apartment before I started school here. I clearly remember that some of the new Saudi students had to stay in motels for more than two months upon their arrival here because they did not find apartments to rent. As result, these Saudis who stay in motels is considered legally as homeless students were affected negatively in the first months because stability is necessary for academic achievement.

I completed all the requirements of the housing agency, then went with one of the agency staff on his truck to see my new apartment. The apartment was about 45 minutes' walk from the Language Institute, and there was a bus station near my apartment with a bus that came at the top of every hour to take students to the campus and downtown. Also, many buses on the campus serve the students and residents, transporting them to all the attractions such as markets like Walmart and Dissmore's IGA. Therefore, I canceled my plan to buy a used car after I saw the effective public transportation in Pullman.

Before the start of school, I finished furnishing the apartment and purchased most of the appliances of a Saudi student who was planning to leave Pullman for another city whom I met through Facebook. I also met some Saudi students during a dinner hosted by the Saudi Club at Washington State University, and the Saudi Club in Pullman was one of the most active Saudi clubs in the U.S. I was surprised by the large number of Saudis in the small city of Pullman because one of the reasons why I chose to study in Pullman is that it is unknown to the Saudis. Accordingly, I would have to speak and practice English all the time because there would not be many Arabic students there. However, my expectations were wrong, and Pullman, at that time, was full of Saudis. There are about 600 Saudi students among a total population of fewer than 35,000 people.

First Week at the Language Institute

The first week of studying was very long for me. I went to my ESL school, the Intensive American Language Center (IALC) at Washington State University. The reception was beautiful on the first day, and the administration provided refreshing drinks and free lunch for the first two days for new students. I think the total number of new students at IALC was 55 students. Most of the new students were from Saudi Arabia, I think about 40 males and females, in addition to 8 Arabs from Oman and 7 Asians. In October 2011, the total number of Saudis at IALC was over 200 students. There were also other Arab students that time, about 20 from Oman, two of them females as I remember, and only one Kuwaiti student. Asian students were a minority in IALC: around 25 students, most of them Chinese. I do not remember students from Africa, India, or South America.

IALC leaders on the morning of the first day also gave us orientation classes, but I could not understand anything because my language was limited. In one of the orientation classes, they brought an officer to teach us about safety and how to reach help from the police departments. Moreover, during that time, IALC brought nurses to vaccinate us as new students against measles, and the new students were tested for Tuberculosis (TB) as well. At noon, IALC leaders gave us cabanas so we could have lunch at the university restaurant for free. In the afternoon, the teachers also walked us through the campus and showed us many essential places for students such as the gym, library, restaurants, and the police department.

On the second day, October 17, 2011, I took an examination in English to determine the right level for me. The Intensive American Language Center (IALC) at Washington State University has six levels:

- Beginner
- Low Intermediate
- Intermediate
- High Intermediate
- Advanced – Undergraduate study preparation (meets WSU language proficiency requirement for undergraduate admission)
- High Advanced – Graduate study preparation (meets WSU language proficiency requirement for graduate study; WSU website).

I have been placed on the second level (Low Intermediate), and most new Saudi students are often placed in the first or second level because Saudi schools do not teach English well enough. Saudis in all English language schools are ranked at the lower level of language because of their limited English language skills. As I have heard from ESL teachers, Saudis generally are better than Asian students in speaking, but Asians are better at writing and reading skills, and reading and writing skills are more essential for college students than speaking. One the third day, we started the first English class at 9 am, and for the first time in my life, I had a female teacher and two female classmates. There were ten students total in my class, all of them Arab, eight from Saudi Arabia and two males from Oman. In this level, we studied three required courses, which were reading/composition, grammar, and listening/speaking. All my teachers at this level were white females. It was a long day for me; at 3 pm I finally finished. My fourth and fifth days were not anything special, except we left school at noon on Friday. I noticed American students and teachers usually appear happier on Friday and sad on Monday. We have the same thing in KSA, where people like the weekend and hate Sunday, which is the first work or study day in the week.

Honeymoon

My first three months were my best time in the United States, and this is common with most individuals when they move to a new culture, as they see everything as new and impressive. This phenomenon is called "honeymoon" by sociologists, and it is the first stage of culture shock where everything seems fantastic. In line with this, I evaluated my honeymoon as excellent. I learned and experienced many things during that time such as studying with Saudi female classmates. Prior to studying with females, I had always been curious about whether women were smarter than men, as women are often more likely to be enrolled in Saudi universities than men. After studying with females, I realized that they were more interested in learning and studying and trying to develop their English than male students.

Additionally, during the honeymoon period of the first three months, I experienced new events related to American culture such as celebrating Halloween, Thanksgiving, and Christmas. I remember the first trip that we went on as students of IALC under the supervision of our teachers to a village close to Pullman to celebrate Halloween. The place was dark, and everyone had disguised themselves with masks. People were deliberately frightened of each other, and sweets, cakes, and chocolate were freely available. I drew on a pumpkin for the first time. After I arrived in Pullman, my Saudi friend and I continued to celebrate Halloween in the city. We went to places that did not close at night and noticed how Americans celebrate this event. Halloween was my first trip with IALC, and I went with them to visit and discover many places around Pullman.

I also celebrated Thanksgiving for the first time. I learned about Thanksgiving and the historical stories associated with it from the school, and I got excited about Thanksgiving. Accordingly, I decided to have a party and cook a turkey a few days before the event. I invited my three females' teachers and their families and all my classmates. All my classmates and two of my teachers came to the party with their families, and I successfully cooked a turkey for the first time. We had a good time celebrating Thanksgiving in my apartment. However, at the end of the party, at about 10 o'clock, I heard an urgent knock on the apartment door while I and some friends were playing cards after the teachers left. I opened the door of the apartment and found a policeman standing there. I was shocked by the presence of the policeman, especially as I had heard a lot of stories about police abuse of Muslims in America. The policeman spoke, but I did not understand what he was saying, so one of my friends who has better English skills than me stepped in to talk with the officer. The officer told my friend that one of the neighbors had complained about the loud sounds and the noise and thus we should not make noise in the evenings. The officer was nice; he smiled at me after he realized that I did not have enough English skills to communicate with him.

On the day of Thanksgiving, IALC linked me to an American family to spend the day with, since it was a holiday. I went to the American family in Pullman to have dinner there and learned about American culture. It was a good time to challenge myself and try to speak English to the Americans. The family hosted two other international students: one from Morocco, and she was a doctoral student at WSU, and the other was from Japan.

The climate differences between the USA and KSA was also an enjoyable experience for me. In some areas of the United States, you can go for long periods without seeing the sun, with periods extending longer than ten days in some cases. Americans, in general, love the sun very much and hate rainy days. This is unlike most Saudis who celebrate the rain because Saudis only see the rain a few times a year, and an entire year may go by without any rain at all. It was also a new experience for me to see the snow and play in it exactly as we see in the movies. The sight of snow falling for the first time was wonderful to me. I went outside to enjoy it, but I realized that I needed a new pair of snow boots. As a result, I went to Moscow ID to buy the boots, which cost me about $100. In addition, I bought a heavy coat that was manufactured by the Columbia Clothing Company. Most Saudis do not like the weather in the U.S., especially in the winter, where the temperature can be lower than 10 F, so they would choose the best states that have reasonable weather like California and Florida.

I experienced the celebration of Christmas for the first time. One of the most beautiful things I saw by the end of my visit was the decoration of streets and buildings before the arrival of Christmas. Moreover, American families usually buy a large Christmas tree and often some smaller ones and place them in the entrances of their homes or in their living rooms. Then they decorate these trees. Further, Americans exchange gifts leading up to the day of the Christmas, put gifts received from family members and friends under the Christmas tree, and ultimately open the gifts on the day of Christmas, which happens on December 25 every year.

The first three months in the United States is the most beautiful time period for me, and the same can be said for many Saudis, because it is the stage of discovering a new country, civilization, and culture. I have attempted in the previous paragraphs to cover the story of my first months in the United States with detail. As I mentioned earlier, I wrote my story not because I am someone special but because I did not find sufficient literature describing the lives of Saudis in America during their first months in the country. Thus, I decided to provide this information to researchers and readers. In the following paragraphs, I will review my stages in the United States summarily.

First year in America

I spent most of my first year in the city of Pullman, at the Language Institute of the Washington State University, with the aim of developing my language as quickly as possible, to get admission to start a master's degree. Before coming to the States, I thought learning English would be a piece of cake in America because I would have to practice all day. However, I found out that learning English is very complex, and terms have many synonyms and have multiple meanings. Learning English was a daunting task for me because I was 24 years old when I joined the language Institute, IALC and also, expectations were too high to learn English from scratch, to reach a level comparable to a post-graduate student in language skills, in a short period of time.

The daily routine during the school days at IALC was going to school in the morning by bus, where my classes start at 9:00 am and end at 3:00 pm, for five days a week, with a one-hour break for lunch. After school, I would take the bus, and headed to my apartment. During my stay in Pullman, I had two homes, the first apartment was far away from my school, and I had to spend 40 minutes on the bus to reach it. Therefore, I moved to another apartment closer to my school so I could reach my school in 15 minutes when walking or in 10 minutes by express bus. In wintertime, I had to take buses because heavy snow and rain made waking very hard for me.

In the evenings, I usually did my homework. My teachers at the institute gave us a lot of homework every day. Accordingly, I needed two to four hours every day to finish my homework. I also decided to follow my teachers' suggestion to watch and listen to radio and TV channels that broadcast in English even when I understood nothing in the first six months. My listening skills were improved by this strategy.

Interacting and practicing English with native speakers were also my priorities, and the tips I gained helped me improve my English in the first year. I used to meet with Americans at least two times a week. First was every Tuesday, when the international office of WSU organizes a program that invites Americans to spend two hours, from noon until 2 p.m., with international students to help these students practice English and explore American culture. Accordingly, I used to go to this gathering with other international students during our lunch break. The second gathering with Americans was at five in the afternoon on Thursday, where young American students at WSU tried to help international students to improve their English skills by organizing a fun class every week; during this class, each American student will chat with four to five international students and discuss many fun topics like sports and movies. I further made friends with several American students during that time. In Pullman, it was easy to make friends because the city is small, and the people are friendly. Also, you can meet these American students many times during the week in public sites, such as the library and the gym. It is also essential to mention that most of those Americans, attempting to help international students, are missionaries who work to convert the beliefs of foreigners into Christianity, particularly Protestantism.

On some weekends, I used my time to rest and meet with other Saudi male friends in Pullman. Sometimes, we went to restaurants, but most of the time, we cooked traditional Saudi food in my apartment. Also, on Saturdays, we often visited Spokane, Wa where there are better places for shopping and dining. I also went about once every two to three weeks to Moscow, ID, for groceries because the prices and taxes there are lower than in Pullman.

Nevertheless, in the first year, I finished three English levels at IALC successfully, which were the second, third and fourth levels; however, the main disadvantage in this institute is that the duration of each level is eight weeks. Students will have a long break after finishing each level, from two to four weeks, particularly in the summertime. As a result, international students need at least three months to complete one level, which is too long for some. For instance, in my situation, I was placed in level two (Low Intermediate). I had planned to apply to a master's program, so I had to complete level six (High Advanced) to be admitted to WSU. Accordingly, I needed at least 15 months to finish my English program, and I was not willing to spend all that time in Pullman.

I decided to leave Pullman and study in Seattle for several reasons. First,I did not get a final acceptance from the College of Education at WSU for the Master of Educational Leadership program because administrators in the department of educational leadership informed me that I have to complete the sixth level or score over 80 in the TOEFL test and then apply for this program. I also noticed at that time that some Saudi students completed their degree at IALC but did not gain acceptance into the graduate programs that they applied for .

Secondly, the language institute in Pullman is recognized only by WSU, unlike my future school in Seattle, which offered an ESL certificate that is recognized by most American universities and equivalent to a TOEFL or IELTS certificate. For example, when intentional students complete level 112 in ESL, they could apply to many universities because these schools have been dealing with ESL students for years, and a student who obtains an ESL certificate meets the English language requirements for graduate applications.The third reason that drives me to leave Pullman us that my score in IELTS and TOEFL were not improving considerably; therefore, I believe I needed to find an American family to live with, so they could help me develop my English skills in a better and faster way.

My Second Year

Before leaving Pullman, I fulfilled the legal procedures for international students who hold F1 student visas. I informed the foreign office at IALA so that they could update my Student and Exchange Visitor Information System (SEVIS). Accordingly, the U.S. Immigration and Customs Enforcement (ICE) knows where international students are located. I also transferred the lease of my apartment to a new tenant, one of my cousins, after I received the landlord's permission. Also, I found an American host family to live with in Seattle through a website called Craigslist. I also asked some American friends in Pullman if they knew families in Seattle that hosted international students, in case I did not like the host family that I found on Craigslist.

When I decided to leave Pullman, I communicated with many language institutes in Seattle, because SACM has regulations for scholarship students who plan to change their ESL school. One of them is that students can change their ESL school only once, and the new school must be in the same state. Accordingly, I chose Seattle, Washington because I found an American family to live with, so I could improve my English faster. Also, by leaving Seattle, I could take the International English Language Testing System (IELTS) many times because when I was at Pullman, I had to travel twice to take the IELTS. The IELTS test is offered only in major cities in the world by supervision from The British Council, unlike the new version of TOEFL, which is called an Internet-based Test (TOEFL IBT) and exists in almost all towns of the USA that have international students. Different reasons led me to leave Pullman; I did not like a small city like Pullman, which does not have enough entertainment places.

My first ESL school choice in Seattle was to study at the language schools of the University of Washington; however, the administrators of the institute informed me that the institute did not have the capacity to accept new students and that many students were on the waiting list. Then, I contacted ESL Seattle, and they gave me admission directly. After getting admission from ESL Seattle, I requested SACM to change schools with my reasons for doing so, and thankfully, SACM officials approved me to move to the new school and emailed me with the financial guarantee to begin the official procedures.

In October 2012, I left Pullman to Seattle by jet, and I rented an economical car from the Seattle airport for two days. Next, I headed directly to meet the host family at their home in the Shoreline district north of Seattle. The family that would host me did not have kids, and there were two Asian American partners in their mid-thirties, we agreed to stay in a private room for me with a shared bathroom with another young American student for 600 dollars a month. The agreement stated that I was to spend no more than ten minutes in the bathroom and should clean it after each use. Other statements in the agreement were that smoking was not allowed in the house or in the backyard and I was not to play with or touch their small lovely dog. Also, the host family would not be responsible for feeding me, so I had to buy and prepare my own food and store it in the part of their giant refrigerator that they had allocated to me. The host father also asked me to give him a copy of my passport and visa for security reasons. I had to accept the agreement because I did not have any other family to stay with in Seattle at the time, renting an apartment in Seattle was expensive, going up to a thousand, and the ESL dorm was full of students. Thus, I had to stay with this family until I found better housing choices.

After I paid my first-month housing payment and got my key and room, I went to the airport to return the rental car. Then, I went back to the house using public transportation, one train and two buses, which took about two hours. I reached Seattle about a week before the first day of school, and I had plenty of time to discover the wonderful city. I also became a member of the LA Fitness Gym which was close to my residence.

ELS

On the first day of the school, which was during November of 2012, I took the early morning bus to Capitol Hill neighborhood where my new school was located. Capitol Hill neighborhood is not far from downtown Seattle, which I classified as one of the best places I ever visited. The trip from my house to the new school (ELS) took about 55 minutes. On the first day as new students, we did a placement test to assign us to a suitable level; I was placed on level 4 out of 12 levels. We started classes on the second day. The first class was at 7:30 am and the last one finished at 3:30 pm. All of my classmates were Saudis except for two who were from Turkey. It is also important to mention that from 2008 to 2015, all ESL programs in the U.S. were full of Saudi students due to the increasing number of scholarships offered by the Saudi government at that time. Tens of thousands of Saudis came to the States to study English before beginning their academic programs in American post-secondary schools.

There are many advantages that make my new school, ELS Seattle branch, a distinctive ESL academy; for example, ELS has accumulated experience in teaching English to non-speakers for more than half a century, and there are dozens of branches of ELS spread over the fifty

American states and other countries such as Saudi Arabia and India. Additionally, ELS provides special curricula, at the Institute, suitable for any level of English, focusing on teaching new vocabulary every day. The main advantage of ELS for international students who plan to study in American higher education institutions is that over 650 universities accept the successful completion of the advanced ELS curriculum as proof of English proficiency. So, international students who complete the 12 levels are not required to take a standardized test that measures English abilities, like TOEFL and IELTS. As is well known, for international students, English standardized tests are a huge obstacle and nightmare because they are difficult tests, and students find it difficult to score high enough to meet the English proficiency requirement for colleges that teach in English.

My daily routine in Seattle

During the year that I lived in Seattle, I had a recurring daily routine where I caught a bus in the early morning five days a week around 6 am to head to my English school. I would spent about an hour on the bus before arriving at the Convention Place Station, the bus station that is close to my school. Note that buses in Seattle are full typically, and it is hard to find a seat during the rush hours. After I finish school at 3:30 pm, I would take the bus again, and the return journey was about 80 minutes. There were no difference in the time I spent on buses between the two distinct places I lived at in the city, because both family houses were located in North Seattle. In the evenings, I did my homework, and generally speaking, ESL teachers give less homework than my old school in Pullman. At night, I usually went to the gym, and at that time, I lost a lot of weight and followed a healthy lifestyle.

Seattle in a major city with many large companies, like Microsoft, Amazon, Boeing, and Starbucks, and thus many people live in the city and the surrounding areas, which is the reason for the persistent traffic on the roads. Accordingly, the city of Seattle created effective public transportation that aimed to encourage people to use trains and buses. As a result, I had no reason to buy a car since the buses served my purpose.

I spent about 3 hours every day on public transportation, including the wait time for buses, and sometimes the buses arrived on time but were full, so we had to wait for another one, which wasted a lot of time each day. My teachers advised me to invest the time spent on or waiting for buses reading something. Accordingly, I subscribed to a local daily newspaper (The Seattle Times), and every morning I read my paper on the bus.

On the weekend, I tried to take more time to rest and sleep in the morning, and in the afternoons, I visited downtown Seattle, which is full of shopping and entertainment places. On some Saturdays, I took the IELTS test. Unlike, TOEFL iBT, the IELTS test still uses paper-and-pencil tests, and students need two times periods to complete the IELTS. The first period went from 9 am until noon and tests students on listening, reading, and writing. After students are finished with writing, they can go and check their names, which are posted on the testing center's corridors, to learn the time of their speaking test. The speaking test's time is usually from 1pm till 9 pm. Consequently, some students will have to wait up to 8 hours to complete all sections of the IELTS test.

Living with an American Family

During my third week in Seattle, I received an email from an American friend who lived in Pullman at that time. He informed me that he found a family that could host me, and he posted all of the relevant information about the potential hosting family. I was hesitant about leaving the house where I lived with an American family of Asian origin because they were nice. However, the couple was busy, so I did not have enough time to visit with them. Also, my American roommate was very friendly but had no time to teach me English. After a long deliberation, I emailed the new host mother, and she invited me to have a pizza dinner with them on the upcoming Friday. So, that Friday, I took the bus at 5 pm from downtown to the Wedgwood neighborhood, north of the city. I reached the house with the help of Google Maps. I met the host mother and we had dinner, then she showed me the house and my room. She was a very nice lady who likes to help international students by hosting them. She also told me her story: she lost her husband years ago and her children were old so no one of her family life with her. Accordingly, she decided to host international students to help them to improve their language skills and adapt to the new-to-them culture. At that time, she also hosted a small family from South Korea.

I liked the nice way this white lady treated me, so I asked her about the price that she would charge me to stay in her house. She asked for only 300 dollars a month, including meals. I was shocked by this offer because I was paying 600 dollars to the Asian family for staying, with no food provided. I asked her, why do you charge only 300 dollars a month when other families charge between 600 to 850 dollars? She responded that she is not looking for money by hosting students; she just wants to help. I agreed to move to her house and take the room in the basement the following week.

Living with the new host family was a real opportunity for me to improve my English ability and experience the way conservative Americans live their lives. The new host mother, Martha, was a very nice, humble lady who treated me like a son. Martha also has a big family and friends who would come and visit her at home; accordingly, I was lucky to know and make friends with her lovely family and great friends. Making friends with Martha's people helped me practice English more, and my new American friends also did their best to encourage me to study harder.

While staying at Martha's home, I was in charge of a few duties, like cleaning the bathroom and washing dishes twice a week. Every evening at 6 pm except on weekends, Martha, the Korean family, and I gathered to have dinner together. Martha and the Korean lady divided the responsibility of making dinner; accordingly, I was lucky to try a variety of tasty Korean foods after that. Korean restaurants have become my favorite, although Korean restaurants are expensive. Every Friday, Martha makes pizza, and Martha is a professional cook who has mastered many varieties of food, especially with baking and sweet food.

I stayed at Martha's home for 13 months, which allowed me to have time to understand American culture in a better way. Martha's friends also taught me American football regulations. However, we would have disagreements because I was a fan of Washington State University's team (the Cougars) and they liked the University of Washington's team, the Huskies. Once, I traveled with Martha and her family to Yakima, WA because they wanted to visit friends there. That was also apple picking season in Yakima, so we went to a farm, and I picked apples for the first time. We also made apple cider, which was tasty. I went with Martha to shows, including plays. To make a long story short, living at Martha's house was a great opportunity for me to improve my English and cultural skills, so I strongly encourage international students to live with American host families.

As I mentioned earlier, I started with level four at the ELS language center in Seattle. I spent about 11 months there until I completed the final English level of ELS, which was called mastery level. During the 11 months, I applied to universities around the States for admission to a master's degree program in educational leadership, and I got conditional admissions, which required a score of 80 points on the TOEFL or 7 on the IELTS. One of the admissions came from Cleveland State University, which accepts the ELS certificate. So, I chose Cleveland to be my next stop in Dreamland.

Summary

In general, it is difficult to mention and write about all the stories I encountered in my first two years in the United States because the details were too numerous. I also may have forgotten some of the events because I do not have a powerful memory and do not write in my diary as some do. In this chapter, I tried to write down the most important events I encountered in my first months in the United States as a foreign student studying English who wanted to master English in order to find acceptance at an American university to study education. In the next chapter, we will learn about critical topics that have affected me during my graduate studies in several colleges of education, particularly in Cleveland, Seattle, and Terre Haute, where I pursued graduate studies.

Chapter Seven: My experience in American higher education institutions

Chapter Seven: My experience in American higher education institutions

After completing the language preparation program, I moved from Seattle, WA, to study for a master's degree at Cleveland University in Ohio beside Lake Erie, which I thought at the time was a sea because I had not enough time to read about Cleveland. Studying in college as an international learner with local classmates is entirely different from being a student at an ESL school, where all learners are not locals and struggle with English. In this chapter, I will inform you about some of the situations that I have encountered in my studies in American universities in general and in short, including my first semester as an international master's student and language and academic challenges I faced. This part also briefly discusses the differences between the educational environments in Saudi Arabia and the US, such as the role of the student in the classroom and the methods of evaluation. In the last part of this chapter, I will provide some tips and suggestions to educational institutions responsible for teaching Saudi students, including American universities.

The first semester

The first semester at the university was a transitional stage for me. After spending almost 24 months in language institutes with foreign students who did not speak fluent English, I found myself in the Education college with local students who did not have language obstacles because their mother tongue was English. In the early months of college, I did not feel well prepared to deal with graduate study tasks because my language skills were not satisfactory. In addition to my deep language problems, I did not know that time about my professors' expectations of me as a graduate student at an American University. For clarification, expectations from the faculty of the College of Education of graduate students are high; consequently, each course challenges students to prepare and read tens of scientific articles and literature before each study. Moreover, professors expect students to read publications with a critical view and not just do a static reading. Accordingly, I believed that I was not up to the challenge to study for postgraduate studies at a university that utilized language that was not my native language, and that failure was closer than ever.

In general, the language barrier was my primary challenge in the first semester and my study journey in American higher education institutions. I had difficulties with English skills, especially reading, writing, and taking notes. I could not handle the reading requirements that professors wanted the students to comprehend. I clearly remember that I spent long hours each day attempting to read and prepare for classes, but often, I did not understand the articles because they contained complex scientific terms beyond my linguistic abilities. In addition to having difficulty reading, I found that the reading materials I studied included topics such as legal and administrative concepts, in which I did not have any background in my mother tongue, which multiplied the difficulties and pressures I was under. Academic writing was also a significant difficulty. Generally, my professors were not satisfied with my level of writing, believing it was way below their expectations for graduate students. Accordingly, they consistently told me to go to the writing center to get help from specialists to improve my essays. Another difficulty I faced was taking notes during lectures. I found it hard to pay attention to the professor and take notes at the same time, so I missed writing down some of the essential thoughts that these scholars were explaining to the class.

I assume that I did not have a big problem with my speaking skills, as the instructors and the students understood what I was trying to say in most cases. Likewise, I did not have a problem with understanding my professors and classmates because Americans generally speak clearly and avoid using complicated words in conversations. During the first semester, I took three courses equivalent to nine-hour credits, and a nine-credit total was the minimum number of hours needed for registration for foreign graduate students holding an F1 (student) visa. Luckily, all my professors during the semester were supportive and inspiring. Therefore, I would like to thank them and tell them that I am really grateful. I would have liked to introduce them here, but out of respect for their privacy, I will not mention their names or titles.

Language difficulties

In general, language skills are divided into four major parts: speaking, listening, reading, and writing. I suspect that my language difficulties were centered more on my reading and writing skills as I did not face a significant challenge with my speaking and listening skills. Overall, my professors and classmates realized what I was saying in most cases. I also had no issues with understanding my teachers and classmates when they were speaking because Americans normally do not use compound words when talking, but they do use them in writing. In this section, I would like to share some challenges that I faced in reading and writing and how I attempted to overcome these challenges.

Reading

Reading was a challenging task for me during my studies in U.S. colleges. My instructors required us as students to prepare for each class by reading no less than between 100 to 200 pages from the expensive textbooks or other scholarly pieces that they wanted us to understand. I did my best to be ready for every class, to be in good intellectual shape, and to play an active learning role in my classes. Reading the lengthy passages took many hours for me because the articles contained vocabulary that was new and complex to me. Therefore, I had to use translation applications to facilitate my comprehension of the reading passages. Some of the professors were somewhat accurate in requiring this, wanting us as students to not only read and understand but also to analyze and critique what we read. Honestly, critical reading skill, in general, was complex and a challenging task that I did not satisfactorily master. The main drawback to not mastering the skill of criticism was my poor English language abilities. Plus, up to this point, I had not read books critically, naively accepting what authors said with no suspicions. Accordingly, I think that one benefit of being educated in an American university is that students learn to have standards of judgment for criticizing written passages instead of believing them foolishly. Finally, I would like to mention that what ultimately helped me understand the texts were advanced technology and applications. For example, I used text-to-speech applications and translation sites, especially Google translation, as I watched some educational videos on YouTube to understand the topics and issues in the American education arena better.

writing Challenges

Writing is one of the most complex skills for human beings; it is a craft that must be learned systematically, unlike speaking, which is a skill that humans acquire naturally and spontaneously. For me, learning to write in a new language at an older age makes learning to write more complicated and difficult to master. In general, my writing skills in English have not been satisfactory for my instructors or for me. I also think that without the assistance of advanced computer applications to correct my spelling and grammar mistakes, writing in English would have been impossible for me. One of the reasons for my low English writing ability, next to the principal cause, which is my humble English skills, is due to the poor preparation provided by language institutes before the start of university courses. I clearly remember that most of our teachers in ESL schools asked us to write about loose topics such as describing a gorgeous site, writing about historical events, or general subjects that have nothing to do with academic matters, rather than anything that required organized reasoning supported by scholarly writing. Consequently, when I began my academic courses in college, I did not have the writing skills expected of university students.

Further, another reason for my poor writing skills may be the difference in the style of writing between Arabic and English. The Arabic script is often abbreviated and does not include many details; as a result, we regularly see Arabic books in small volumes, and the number of pages does not exceed 150 even with a bigger font. In contrast, the English language follows a more clearly written method than Arabic scripts by applying similar formations, including introduction, body, and conclusion. Writing in English requires adding details and explaining many points, so we see essential books in English that exceed 400 pages using a small font. Because I was used to writing in Arabic, I wrote with a kind of abbreviation without mentioning many examples and details about topics that I was writing about. Accordingly, most of my professors habitually asked me to rewrite parts of my articles and essays in a more understandable and detailed way and to mention tons of examples and citations. Overall, my writing was not satisfactory to me nor to my professors, who always felt a bit dissatisfied with my articles and essays; however, it has become a little better since I received help from the writing center staff, who assisted me in rewriting the sentences in an appropriate way for academic writing.

Relationship with Professors

I believe one of the most critical factors for the success of my academic experience in the United States was the help given by my professors. Luckily, the majority of the professors who taught and supervised me while I was studying in the States as an international student possessed many honorable values such as humility and supportiveness. For the most part, my professors apprehended that other non-native English speakers and I encountered difficulty with language; accordingly, they allowed us to use dictionaries to translate terms that we did not understand, whether during regular classes or exams.

Further, communication with professors was accessible during weekdays through electronic communications. Students can save a significant amount of time reaching their instructors via phone or email, eliminating the need to meet with teachers to speak about assignments. I went to the professors' offices to talk about a particular subject only a very few times; I usually emailed them and sometimes called or texted them directly. The good thing about these professors is that they respond fast, within 24 hours, despite their busyness, and I appreciate their efforts to assist students. I would like to state the names of all my professors in this section, thanking them and telling them how grateful I am to them, but in respect of their privacy, I will not mention their names.

Classmates

When I was a graduate student, most of my local classmates were older and already had families and full-time jobs, especially in school fields. Most of the classmates that I met were friendly and kind to other Saudi classmates and me. I worked with many locals to complete academic projects for our classes, and they were supportive and committed to the project with me. However, I could not develop a friendship with my local classmates; I always had shallow relationships with them. I believe multiple reasons made it hard for me to develop familiarity with my classmates. The primary reason is that we did not share the same values and cultural backgrounds. Throughout my time living in the United States, I have found that many new immigrants, including Arabs, Muslims, Indians, and Hispanics, report through conversations their difficulties building reliable and genuine friendships with Americans. It essential here to distinguish between "normal" Americans and Americans engaged in Christianization. Americans who work in churches and evangelization are very close to migrant communities and foreign-student groups compared to average Americans. These missionaries are attempting to spread the teachings of their faith to these "outsiders" in the local community; as a result, most of the international students have a good relationship with the American missionaries who work on campuses.

Syllabus

The syllabus or program plan is one of the new concepts that I learned for the first time in my life in the U.S. educational setting. Syllabuses usually include details and descriptive pieces of information about all aspects of the courses such as reading materials, assignments, expectations, university rules, course outcomes, and—the most important for many students—grading and evaluation. From my perspective, syllabuses let students know from the first class in each course the goals that they need to accomplish; thus, there will be no surprises for students, and this makes them concentrate on their learning. My professors customarily spend the first class reviewing, so all students have the opportunity to ask when they do not understand something in the syllabus. Lastly, I urge Saudi schools and universities to design syllabuses for their classes because they will reduce permanent problems between professors and students, especially with regard to evaluation.

Grading

The professors and instructors who taught me in the U.S. higher-education institutions had different approaches to grading. The first was the traditional way of evaluation by administering pen-and-paper exams. Students would take two exams, the midterm and the final, and are required to pass these exams as the only indicator for evaluation. I believe that the professors who applied exam strategies to my classmates and I underestimated the importance of the role of the students and their active participation in the classroom. The second group of professors used several different methods of assessment, including examinations, written articles, reports, and presentations. The third group of instructors applied new techniques of evaluation, such as focusing on the effectiveness of classroom participation, writing research and articles, doing projects with other classmates, and delivering presentations. I personally prefer the third approach to grading because the educational effects remain with the learner for longer because the learner acquires many new skills during these sessions.

Digital libraries at American universities

One of the crucial factors for my success at U.S. universities was the help of librarians. The librarians enabled me to access the references and research that I needed to complete projects related to my studies. Modern American libraries are digital and smart because they are linked to massive databases; as a result, researchers do not have to physically go to a library to find a book or a piece of research. When I was a student, I did not physically go to the university library very often; I always benefitted from a virtual site. I ordered books and research online and got most of them in digital format. Sometimes, when a library did not have a book in digital format, they sent the book via mail. Because of the great services that researchers at U.S. universities get, it is not surprising that American universities and their research centers publish most of the research in the world.

Students role in learning

In contrast to my experiences in the educational environments in Saudi Arabia, students play an active role in most of the study programs I have studied during my sojourn in the United States, either in language institutes or postgraduate programs. When I was studying in schools or even at a university in Saudi Arabia, most of my instructors adopted the old style of teaching, which is a one-way teaching strategy. Accordingly, instructors need to explain every element of the textbooks with low or no participation from students. As students, our role was, in most cases, copy what teachers write on the whiteboards, do homework, and pass exams. In KSA's schools, students are not expected to play active roles in their learning; therefore, the teachers are less likely to encourage their students to ask questions, give presentations and do project work, write reports, and participate in sports, and social activities;, no debating or advocating skills are encouraged either.

As a result, I faced difficulty when I moved to study in the U.S. institutions not only with the language and cultural obstacles but also with teachers' expectations from students. In the first period, I tended to be silent in the classrooms, just like when I was in Saudi schools, and I ask a few questions at some point. However, I noticed that some of my professors were pushing me to participate by asking me questions directly to me, such as what my opinion about educational issues and events was. Consequently, I realized early that I needed to challenge myself and be among active learners. I was an active and excellent student in most of my classes in the U.S. Fortunately, I was quick to adapt to the American study environment despite the difficulties I faced in asking valuable questions and giving proper presentations in a new language.

Unfortunately, the educational system in Saudi Arabia and other Arab countries generally concentrates on developing the low skills of the learners, such as recalling and understanding the information posted in student textbooks. At the same time, these schools ignore higher learning skills, such as critical thinking, analysis, and creativity. On the opposite side, in many of the classes that

I attended at American universities, professors purposely aimed to challenge their students to ensure that they learn to think critically and creatively. For instance, educators asked us to critique the writing pieces of some scholars in education, administration, and psychology. Moreover, some professors asked us to imagine effective schools in the next half of this century. I worked hard to develop this higher level of thinking; however, I did not feel satisfied doing things that required higher intelligence abilities for two reasons: lack of preparation to deal with higher education skills and language barrier. Schools that I studied at did not prepare me to develop these skills when I was young. Also, because of the language limitations, I could not comprehend the scholarly articles deeply, resulting in insufficient critiques. Therefore, I call the Saudi schools to promote higher learning skills just like the advanced education systems in the first-world countries and to intensify the teaching of English to Saudi students in public schools.

Suggestions

At the end of my educational journey in the United States, which began with learning English, then studying for a master's degree, and finally getting my Ph.D., I would like to share some recommendations with the educational authorities responsible for teaching Saudi students, including language institutes, leaders and professors of U.S. colleges, SACM, and schools in Saudi Arabia. I believe the mentioned educational administrations work well generally. However, there are opportunities for these organizations to advance their levels of service to Saudi students and reduce the difficulties faced by Saudi Arabian students in post-secondary American institutions.

ESL

Saudi students who earn scholarships from the Saudi government regularly spend a period of one to two years at institutes of English for non-native speakers in the United States, and these students are full-time learners who intensively study English to prepare to become college students in the U.S. During my experience at language learning institutes, my teachers and administrators made a great effort to help us learn English, including spending a long time and a lot of energy to teach us the correct ways pronounce and understand new terms. Although the two language schools I attended were unique and effective learning centers, I imagine that there are aspects at these two and other English institutes that should improve for the benefit of non-native learners.

I have several beneficial tips that language institutes should apply in my view to prepare Saudi students, in particular, and foreigners, in general, to be ready for the challenges of higher education in the United States. The first advice for language institutes to adequately prepare Saudi and international students for the academic challenges in higher education is to intensify the use of academic vocabulary or formal concepts and to minimize using slang; slang words are still important but students can learn slang later on. The second advice is to use academic curricula and books close to the curriculum that college students learn from, especially at advanced levels, in language institutes. As a result, international students will not be shocked when they see the giant books professors usually ask their students to read for university courses.

The other advice for ESL schools is to apply a system similar to what colleges use in terms of expectations, attendance, and discipline regulations. There are high expectations for college students to be responsible and self-mentors in terms of coming on time for classes, delivering duties and projects on time, as well as being active learners inside classes. Colleges also apply strict rules of discipline in cases of misconduct, such as cheating and plagiarism. Therefore, I believe that preparing these groups of non-local students in ESL schools in standards used in American institutions of higher education would help reduce many misconduct issues for these students when they go to college. Also, one of the reasonable steps that ESL schools need to concentrate on is intensifying academic reading courses so that students will have the opportunity to learn new terms and challenge their ability to read books as well as scholarly articles published in English.

    The most crucial point is to intensify teaching Saudi students and foreigners at language institutes academic writing skills that require more effort to master (e.g., focusing on a topic, creating a useful outline, preparing examples, and developing writing structure skills). It is also beneficial for students to be trained to use references in their articles and writing assignments at the language institutes as well as follow the same writing styles that colleges use such as the American Psychological Association (APA) and Modern Language Association (MLA) formats. As a result, these groups of students will be familiar with the methods of writing when they move to study at American higher education institutions. In the end, I would want the leaders of ESL institutions to encourage the local community to associate with non-local students. That way, international students would learn more about American culture and have more of a chance to enhance their language proficiency by practicing with native speakers.

Universities

From my experience in four American universities and two language schools, I can say that many departments, administrators, and instructors should invest in developing and improving on skills around lessening the stress felt by international students, including Saudis. I believe that many of the international student centers at the universities where I studied need to develop and offer more services and information to international students. One of the suggestions that such centers could offer is educating international students about American culture in general, such as the rules around drinking and eating appropriately according to American culture and respecting spaces in elevators. Also, these centers could educate students about what American professors expect from students and vice versa. International students come from different parts of the world with many cultures and languages, so many of these students, including myself, do not know the expectations required of us as students in classrooms and what our rights and duties are. Also, the leadership in foreign student centers tend to have a great cultural background because they deal with international students intensively and directly. Thus, it makes sense for these leaders to educate local students and professors about the cultural aspects of international students and ways to help them succeed in American educational institutions. Global student centers can create booklets or schedule lectures on the cultural aspects regarding non-local students, such as understanding that some Saudi female students prefer to not deal with male students in most cases for cultural reasons. All in all, international centers can take on a more active role in serving non-local students and helping them with cultural integration.

I also advise the leaders of American universities to conduct training workshops for professors to instruct them in appropriate ways to teach and deal with foreign students. Many teachers have never taught students who do not speak English as their first language, so these teachers do not realize the difficulties these international learners face in understanding the course materials. Therefore, it is beneficial to educate instructors about the difficulties foreign students experience academically and share the most appropriate teaching and evaluation methods for these learners. For example, in these workshops, teachers can be trained not to speak too fast and avoid complex concepts so all students can understand lectures, including non-local students who struggle with English.

Additionally, professors should be educated on the sensitive cultural aspects of some foreign students, including Saudis. For example, many Saudi women do not prefer to shake hands with men, so it is proper for instructors to understand these details so that no misunderstanding occurs. Some professors, on some occasions, also bring meals to their students that contain meat, but Muslims cannot have these meals for religious reasons. Accordingly, I believe that instructing professors on the cultural aspects of their foreign students contributes well to improving the educational climate in US educational institutions that contain foreign learners.

SACM

The Saudi Arabian Cultural Mission (SACM) in relation to the United States as a representative of the Ministry of Education does a great job in serving Saudi students by supervising their education, depositing the monthly salaries of the students in their American bank accounts, and paying tuition for American colleges on behalf of Saudi scholarship students. The SACM also has the potential to play a more dynamic role in the support of Saudi students in the United States and maximize the likelihood of success for these Saudis. One of the ideas that the SACM should apply is the dissemination of more statistical information about Saudi students in the US. The SACM has a massive database on Saudi students since all Saudi scholarship students are required to send each semester's official transcript about their grades. Therefore, the SACM should make a detailed annual report of Saudi students that contains a lot of information, including average scores for Saudi students, success and repetition rates, student specialties, universities where they study, and drop-out percentages. Dissemination of statistical information about Saudi students will lead researchers and specialists to analyze the data and identify the imbalances to be repaired to ensure the success of the most significant number of Saudis educated abroad.

It is worthy for the SACM to take action in educating leaders and professors at American universities where Saudis are studying the cultural aspects of these students. Arab culture, including Saudi culture, is very different from Western culture. Accordingly, it is beneficial to teach American professors about the cultures' differences to try to adapt, mainly in regards to religious differences. For example, Saudis, as Muslim students, pray five times a day at specific times. Unlike Christianity, prayer times are not flexible, and some events, like lectures, overlap with prayer times. Consequently, it would be a noble act for professors to give a short break for students during class so that Muslim students can perform their prayers. Also, some Saudi women do not want to sit next to or work with male classmates for religious and cultural reasons. Americans teachers need to be made aware of their Saudi students' culture. The best agency to do that is SACM. The SACM can educate professors and leaders of American universities about Saudi culture through several methods, such as holding conferences and meetings, printing books about the Saudis and their culture and distributing them to universities, or producing an educational film.

It is hoped that SACM will also educate Saudi students more professionally about American laws and immigration regulations, so Saudis will not be exposed to legal problems during their presence in American territory. Further, SACM could improve in teaching new Saudi students in the United States about American cultural aspects, such as the importance of time. This concept represents a vast difference between Arab and American cultures; Americans commit seriously to their times of study and work. On the other hand, Arabs, including Saudis, do not care much about being on time for their classes or work. Therefore, it is essential to teach new Saudi students more about the expectations for students and individuals according to their host culture. I suggested that SACM should produce educational films on culture, laws, and education in the United States to make it easier for Saudis to understand these topics in relation to the host nation. I strongly believe that, with the application of the tips mentioned in this section, the SACM will have significantly contributed to giving Saudi students more opportunities to succeed in higher education institutions in the United States.

Tips for the Saudi Ministry of Education

Unlike most western country educational systems, the educational system in Saudi Arabia is central, so the Ministry of Education is the supreme authority and reference of all public schools in the country. Also, all public-school students learn and read the same books. For instance, students in the fifth grade in a public school in Riyadh use identical books as other students in the same level of education in the city of Hafr al-Batin; this is the so-called national curriculum. My view on the centralization of the educational system in my country is not crucial in this book; therefore, I would like to deliver some suggestions to public schools that are preparing their students better to be global learners who can compete with other students from other nations in the 21st century. Competition is one of the features of this century; accordingly, we see people, giant companies, and countries fighting to get prosperous opportunities; therefore, public schools need to prepare their students to be competitors; individuals like to challenge themselves.

One of the tips offered to public schools in Saudi Arabia that makes Saudi students able to study in American universities successfully is the development of a curriculum and the methods of teaching English. Public schools in KSA teach English to students from the 4th grade until the last year of high school, which is the 12th grade; however, most Saudi school students still cannot pass the standardized tests that measure English abilities for non-native speakers, such as TOEFL or IELTS. Accordingly, Saudi students who move to the USA to study at universities have to spend a lot of time studying English again before being accepted into colleges because public schools in KSA do not teach English effectively and our skills in this language are weak.

One of the tips I would like the Ministry to apply is to intensify the teaching of reading and writing in English to reduce the language barrier for students who want to study in English-speaking universities or abroad in countries such as the United States.

I also encourage the leaders of the Ministry of Education to re-train teachers each year on the modern teaching methods that make students the center of learning, and train teachers on ways to develop the capabilities of their students, including the development of creative and critical skills. Finally, I would like the Ministry to emphasize in its schools the importance of applying disciplinary policies on students in all aspects, including coming to school on time, behavioral issues, and attendance because American universities have high expectations from their students. With the implementation of these suggestions, it is hoped that public schools in KSA will be able to help their students have a better chance to flourish in American institutions of higher education.

Summary

The chapter presented, in brief, some essential points of my educational journey at American universities. Language problems were my main academic obstacle, and language issues severely limited my abilities in many areas. At the same time, my professors provided me with a lot of support and assistance and were an essential factor in my academic success at American universities. In the last part of this chapter, I also tried to give some advice to those responsible for educating Saudi students to ensure the success of as many Saudis as possible in the US universities in the future.

References

"A Guide To The United States' History Of Recognition, Diplomatic, And Consular Relations, By Country, Since 1776: Morocco". state.gov. Retrieved March 26, 2016.

Abdel Razek, A. N. A. (2012). An exploration of the case of Saudi students' engagement success and self-efficacy at a Mid-Western American University (Doctoral dissertation, University of Akron). Retrieved from http://rave.ohiolink.edu/etdc/view?acc_num=akron1337282450

Al Musaiteer, S. S. (2015). Saudi students' experience of intercultural communication (Master thesis, University of Akron).

Al-Khedair, K. S. (1978). Cultural perception and attitudinal differences among Saudi Arabian male college students in the United States.

Al-Shehry, A. (1989). An investigation of the financial and academic problems perceived by Saudi graduate students while they are studying in the United States (Doctoral dissertation)

Bai, J. (2016). Perceived support as a predictor of acculturative stress among international students in the United States. *Journal of International Students*, 6(1), 93-106.

Caldwell, J. D. (2013). *Examining the experiences and adjustment challenges of Saudi Arabian students in the California state university system*. California State University, Fresno.

Can, A. (2015). *An Examination of the Relationship Between Adjustment Problems, Homesickness, Perceived Discrimination and Psychological Wellbeing Among*

International Students(Doctoral dissertation, Ohio University).

Constantine, M.G., Okazaki, S., & Utsey, S.O. (2004). Self-concealment, social self-efficacy, acculturative stress, and depression in African, 105 Asian, and Latin American international college students. American Journal of Orthopsychiatry, 74, 230-241

Daller, M. H., & Phelan, D. (2013). Predicting international student study success. *Applied Linguistics Review, 4*(1), 173-193.

Gautam, C. C., Lowery, C. I., Mays, C. C., & Durant, D. G. (2016). Challenges for global learners: A qualitative study of the concerns and difficulties of international students. *Journal of International Students, 6*(2), 501-526.

Gay, L. R., Mills, E. G., & Airasian, P. (2012). Education research: Competence for analysis and application. *Ohio: Merrill Publishing Co. Ltd.*

Geary, D. (2016). How do we get people to interact? International students and the American experience. *Journal of International Students, 6*(2), 527-541.

Ghaffari, N. (2009). Beyond 9/11: American muslim youth transcending pedagogies of stigma to resilience. Dissertation Abstracts International: Section A. Humanities and Social Sciences. Retrieved from http://search.proquest.com/docview/622102560?accountid=15099

Hofer, J. V. (2009). The identification of issues serving as barriers to positive educational experiences for Saudi Arabian students studying in the state of Missouri. Available from ProQuest Dissertations and Theses database.

Jammaz, A. I. A. (1972). SAUDI STUDENTS IN THE UNITED STATES: A STUDY OF THEIR ADJUSTMENT PROBLEMS.

Johnson, B., & Christensen, L. (2008). Educational research: Quantitative, qualitative, and mixed approaches (p. 34). Thousand Oaks, CA: Sage Publications.

Koys, D. (2010). GMAT versus alternatives: Predictive validity evidence from Central Europe and the middle east. *Journal of Education for Business*, *85*, 180–185.

Krausz, J., Schiff, A., Schiff, J., & Hise, J. V. (2005). The impact of TOEFL scores on placement and performance of international students in the initial graduate accounting class. *Accounting Education, 14*(1), 103-111. doi:10.1080/0963928042000256671

Kusek, W. A. (2015). Evaluating the struggles with international students and local community participation. *Journal of International Students, 5*(2), 121-131. Retrieved from http://ojed.org/index.php/jis/article/view/429

Kutintara, I., & Min, S. (2016). Sport participation and US sport culture influences among college-age international students. *Journal of Multidisciplinary Research, 8*(2), 49-60.

Lefdahl-Davis, E. M., & Perrone-McGovern, K. M. (2015). The cultural adjustment of Saudi women international students: A qualitative examination. Journal of Cross-Cultural Psychology, 46(3), 406-434.

Lichtman, M. (2006). Qualitative research in education: A user's guide (pp. 7-8). Thousand Oaks, CA: Sage Publication

Lin, S. Y., & Scherz, S. D. (2014). Challenges facing Asian international graduate students in the US: Pedagogical considerations in higher education. *Journal of International Students, 4*(1), 16–33. Retrieved from https://files.eric.ed.gov/fulltext/ej1100337.pdf

Liu, D. (2016). Strategies to promote Chinese international students' school performance: Resolving the challenges in American higher education. *Asian-Pacific Journal of Second and Foreign Language Education, 1* ,1-8.

Long, D. E., & Maisel, S. (2010). *The Kingdom of Saudi Arabia*. Gainesville, FL: University Press of Florida.

Macionis, J., & Gerber, L. (2010). Sociology. (7th ed.). Toronto, Canada: Pearson Education.

Martirosyan, N. N., Eunjin Hwang1, E., & Wanjohi, R. W. (2015). Impact of English proficiency on academic performance of International Students. *Journal of International Students, 5*(1), 60-71. Retrieved from https://files.eric.ed.gov/fulltext/ej1052835.pdf

Matusitz, J. (2015). The acculturative experience of French students in a southwestern university apartment complex in the United States. *Journal of Human Behavior in the Social Environment, 25*(3), 261-274

McFarland, J., Hussar, B., Zhang, J., Wang, X., Wang, K., Hein, S., Diliberti, M., Forrest Cataldi, E., Bullock Mann, F., and Barmer, A. (2019). The Condition of Education 2019 (NCES 2019-144). U.S. Department of Education. Washington, DC: National Center for Education Statistics. Retrieved [date] from https://nces.ed.gov/pubsearch/pubsinfo.asp?pubid=2019144.

McMurtrie, B., Bollag, B., Brender, A., del Castillo, D., Cheng, M., & Overland, M. A. (2001). Arab students in U.S. head home, citing growing hostility. Chronicle of Higher Education, 48, A42.

Melius, C. (2017). Saudi Student Integration in Southeastern US Higher Education Institutions: A Study on the Impact of Academic, Social, and Cultural Adjustments Related to Academic Success.

Rabia, A., & Hazza, M. (2017). Undergraduate Arab International Students' Adjustment to US Universities. *International Journal of Higher Education, 6*(1), 131-139.

Sandekian, R. E., Weddington, M., Birnbaum, M., & Keen, J. K. (2015). A narrative inquiry into academic experiences of female Saudi graduate students at a comprehensive doctoral university. *Journal of Studies in International Education, 19*(4), 360-378.

Shaw, D. L. (2010). Bridging differences: Saudi arabian students reflect on their educational experiences and share success strategies (Order No. 3401195). Available from Ethnic NewsWatch; ProQuest Dissertations & Theses Global. (89188218). Retrieved from http://search.proquest.com/docview/89188218?accountid=14556

Smoking in the Kingdom of Saudi Arabia: Findings from the Saudi Health Interview Survey (2014) the Ministry of Health in Saudi Arabia. http://www.healthdata.org/sites/default/files/files/Projects/KSA/Smoking-KSA-Findings-from-the-Saudi-Health-Interview-Survey.pdf

Urias, D. A., & Yeakey, C. C. (2005). International students and US border security. The National Education Association Higher Education Journal, 1, 187-198. Retrieved from http://www.nea.org/assets/img/pubthoughtandaction/taa_05_18.pdf

Waite, M. (Ed.). (2007). *Oxford dictionary and thesaurus*. American Chemical Society.

Yakaboski, T., Perez-Velez, K., & Almutairi, Y. (2016). Collectivists' decision-making: Saudi Arabian graduate students' study abroad choices. *Journal of International Students 2017 Vol 7 Issue 1, 7*(1), 94-112.

APPENDIX

TOP HOST DESTINATIONS, 2001 & 2018

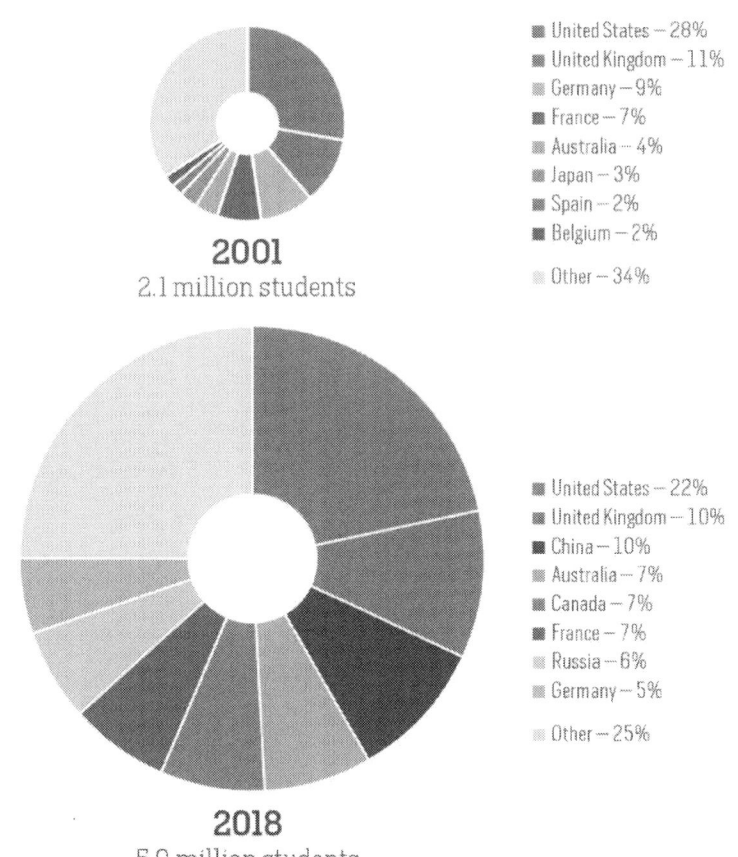

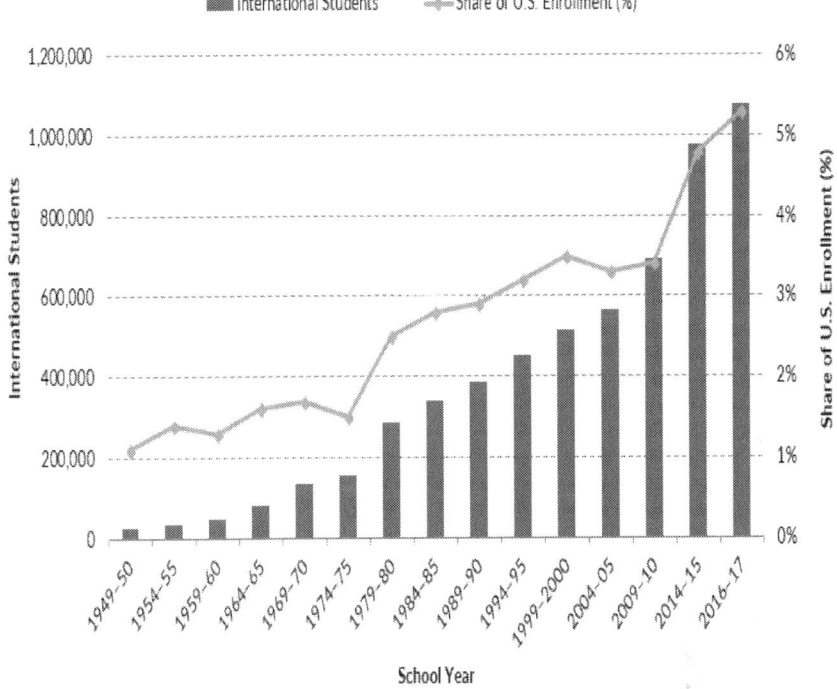

Primary Source of Funding

INTERNATIONAL STUDENT DATA
FROM THE 2018 OPEN DOORS® REPORT

Academic Year: 2017/18

Funding Source	Value	% of Total	Academic Level			
			Undergraduate	Graduate	Non-Degree	OPT
Total Students	1,094,792	100	442,746	382,953	65,631	203,462
Personal and Family	641,318	58.6	82.3	59.9	72.6	0.0
U.S. College or University*	172,531	15.8	8.1	33.8	11.5	0.0
Foreign Government or University	56,549	5.2	7.7	3.8	11.9	0.0
Foreign Private Sponsor	6,301	0.6	0.6	0.9	0.8	0.0
Current Employment	205,642	18.8	0.0	0.5	0.3	100.0
U.S. Government	2,597	0.2	0.1	0.4	0.8	0.0

Academic Level
Undergraduate

Source of Funding
- Personal and Family
- U.S. College or University*
- Foreign Government or University
- Current Employment
- Foreign Private Sponsor
- International Organization
- U.S. Government
- U.S. Private Sponsor
- Other Sources

*Funding from U.S. college or universities includes teaching and research assistantships, which are often federal government research grants disbursed to the student through the institution.

Suggested citation: Institute of International Education. (2018). "International Students by Primary Source of Funding, 2015/16 - 2017/18." Open Doors Report on International Educational Exchange. Retrieved from http://www.iie.org/opendoors

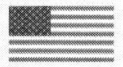  

opendoors® 2018 "Fast Facts"

INTERNATIONAL STUDENTS IN THE U.S.

NEW INTERNATIONAL STUDENT ENROLLMENT

Year	Count	
2012/13	250,920	New international student
2013/14	270,128	enrollment — students enrolling for
2014/15	293,766	the first time at a U.S. institution in
2015/16	300,743	fall 2017 — decreased by 6.6% over
2016/17	290,836	the previous year.
2017/18	**271,738**	

INTERNATIONAL STUDENT TRENDS*

In 2017/18, the number of international students in the U.S. increased by 1.5% to 1,094,792 students.

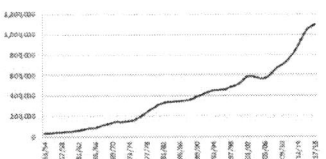

	Total int'l students	% change	U.S. higher education total**	% int'l
2006/07	582,984	3.2	17,672,000	3.3
2007/08	623,805	7.0	18,248,000	3.4
2008/09	671,616	7.7	19,103,000	3.5
2009/10	690,923	2.9	20,428,000	3.4
2010/11	723,277	4.7	20,550,000	3.5
2011/12	764,495	5.7	20,625,000	3.7
2012/13	819,644	7.2	21,253,000	3.9
2013/14	886,052	8.1	21,216,000	4.2
2014/15	974,926	10.0	20,300,000	4.8
2015/16	1,043,839	7.1	20,264,000	5.2
2016/17	1,078,822	3.4	20,185,000	5.3
2017/18	**1,094,792**	**1.5**	**19,831,000**	**5.5**

**Data from the National Center of Education Statistics*

TOP U.S. STATES HOSTING INTERNATIONAL STUDENTS*

		2016/17	2017/18	% change
1	California	156,879	161,942	3.2
2	New York	118,424	121,260	2.4
3	Texas	85,118	84,348	-0.9
4	Massachusetts	62,926	68,192	8.4
5	Illinois	52,225	53,362	2.2
6	Pennsylvania	51,129	51,817	1.3
7	Florida	45,718	46,518	1.7
8	Ohio	38,680	37,583	-2.8
9	Michigan	34,296	34,049	-0.7
10	Indiana	30,600	29,994	-2.0

Note: Percent distribution may not total 100.0 due to rounding
*Numbers include both enrolled international students and international students on Optional Practical Training

The Institute of International Education (IIE) has conducted an annual census of international students in the U.S. since its founding in 1919. Known as the Open Doors Report since 1954, and supported by the Bureau of Educational and Cultural Affairs of the U.S. Department of State since 1972, the report provides detailed data on student flows into and out of the U.S. Visit us online at http://www.iie.org/opendoors.

TOP PLACES OF ORIGIN OF INTERNATIONAL STUDENTS*

		2016/17	2017/18	% of Total	% Change
	World TOTAL	1,078,822	1,094,792	100.0	1.5
1	China	350,755	363,341	33.2	3.6
2	India	186,267	196,271	17.9	5.4
3	South Korea	58,663	54,555	5.0	-7.0
4	Saudi Arabia	52,611	44,432	4.1	-15.5
5	Canada	27,065	25,909	2.4	-4.3
6	Vietnam	22,438	24,325	2.2	8.4
7	Taiwan	21,516	22,454	2.1	4.4
8	Japan	18,780	18,753	1.7	-0.1
9	Mexico	16,835	15,468	1.4	-8.1
10	Brazil	13,089	14,620	1.3	11.7
11	Nepal	11,607	13,270	1.2	14.3
12	Iran	12,643	12,783	1.2	1.1
13	Nigeria	11,710	12,693	1.2	8.4
14	United Kingdom	11,489	11,450	1.0	-0.3
15	Turkey	10,586	10,520	1.0	-0.6
16	Kuwait	9,825	10,190	0.9	3.7
17	Germany	10,169	10,042	0.9	-1.2
18	France	8,814	8,802	0.8	-0.1
19	Indonesia	8,778	8,650	0.8	-1.4
20	Venezuela	8,540	8,371	0.8	-2.0
21	Malaysia	8,247	8,271	0.8	0.3
22	Colombia	7,982	7,976	0.7	-0.1
23	Pakistan	7,015	7,537	0.7	7.4
24	Bangladesh	7,143	7,496	0.7	4.9
25	Spain	7,164	7,489	0.7	4.5

TOP U.S. INSTITUTIONS HOSTING INTERNATIONAL STUDENTS, 2017/18*

1	New York University	New York	NY	17,552
2	University of Southern California	Los Angeles	CA	16,075
3	Northeastern University - Boston	Boston	MA	14,905
4	Columbia University	New York	NY	14,615
5	Arizona State University - Tempe	Tempe	AZ	13,459
6	University of Illinois - Urbana-Champaign	Champaign	IL	13,445
7	University of California - Los Angeles	Los Angeles	CA	12,017
8	Purdue University - West Lafayette	West Lafayette	IN	11,044
9	University of California - San Diego	La Jolla	CA	9,883
10	Boston University	Boston	MA	9,742
11	University of Texas - Dallas	Richardson	TX	9,713
12	University of California - Berkeley	Berkeley	CA	9,331
13	University of Washington	Seattle	WA	8,902
14	Pennsylvania State University - University Park	University Park	PA	8,836
15	Carnegie Mellon University	Pittsburgh	PA	8,604
16	University of Michigan - Ann Arbor	Ann Arbor	MI	8,442
17	University of California - Irvine	Irvine	CA	7,902
18	Michigan State University	East Lansing	MI	7,624
19	Indiana University - Bloomington	Bloomington	IN	7,343
20	University of California - Davis	Davis	CA	7,316

ACADEMIC LEVEL TRENDS OF INTERNATIONAL STUDENTS

	Undergraduate	% change	Graduate	% change	Non-degree	% change	OPT	% change
2013/14	370,724	9.0	329,854	6.0	79,477	8.1	105,997	11.7
2014/15	398,824	7.6	362,228	9.8	93,567	17.8	120,287	13.5
2015/16	427,313	7.1	383,935	6.0	85,093	-9.1	147,498	22.6
2016/17	439,019	2.7	391,124	1.9	72,984	-14.2	175,695	19.1
2017/18	442,746	0.8	382,953	-2.1	65,831	-10.1	203,462	15.8

INTERNATIONAL STUDENTS IN THE U.S. (CONT'D)

PRIMARY SOURCE OF FUNDING*	2017/18	% of total
Personal and Family	641,316	58.6
Current Employment	205,642	18.8
U.S. College or University	172,531	15.8
Foreign Government or University	56,549	5.2
Foreign Private Sponsor	6,301	0.6
U.S. Private Sponsor	2,857	0.2
U.S. Government	2,597	0.2
International Organization	1,598	0.1
Other Source	5,598	0.5
TOTAL INT'L STUDENTS	**1,094,792**	**100.0**

SELECTED FIELDS OF STUDY*	2016/17	2017/18	% of total	% change
Engineering	230,711	232,710	21.3	0.9
Business and Management	200,754	196,054	17.9	-2.3
Math and Computer Science	167,180	186,003	17.0	11.3
Social Sciences	83,046	83,708	7.6	0.8
Physical and Life Sciences	76,838	78,700	7.2	2.4
Fine and Applied Arts	61,508	63,795	5.8	3.7
Health Professions	34,395	35,169	3.2	2.3
Intensive English	30,309	25,845	2.4	-14.7
Communications and Journalism	21,913	22,824	2.1	4.2
Education	17,990	17,615	1.6	-2.1
Humanities	17,561	17,040	1.6	-3.0
Legal Studies and Law Enforcement	15,306	16,894	1.5	10.4
Agriculture	12,602	12,473	1.1	-1.0

U.S. STUDENTS STUDYING ABROAD

332,727 U.S. students studied abroad for academic credit in 2016/17, an increase of 2.3% over the previous year.

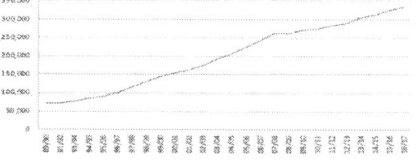

TOP FIVE MAJOR FIELDS OF STUDY	2015/16	2016/17	% of total	% change
Science, Technology, Engineering & Math	81,848	85,786	25.8	4.8
Business	68,122	68,757	20.7	0.9
Social Sciences	55,602	57,081	17.2	2.7
Foreign Language & Int'l Studies	23,917	24,199	7.3	1.1
Fine or Applied Arts	22,328	21,044	6.3	-5.8

RACE/ETHNICITY	2006/07	2011/12	2016/17
White	81.9	76.4	70.8
Hispanic or Latino(a)	6.0	7.6	10.2
Asian or Pacific Islander	6.7	7.7	8.2
Black or African-American	3.5	5.3	6.1
Multiracial	1.2	2.5	4.0
American Indian or Alaska Native	0.5	0.5	0.4
TOTAL U.S. STUDENTS ABROAD	**241,791**	**283,332**	**332,727**

DESTINATIONS		2015/16	2016/17	% of total	% change
1	United Kingdom	39,140	39,851	12.0	1.8
2	Italy	34,894	35,366	10.6	1.4
3	Spain	29,975	31,230	9.4	4.2
4	France	17,214	16,462	4.9	-4.4
5	Germany	11,900	12,585	3.8	5.8
6	China	11,688	11,910	3.6	1.9
7	Ireland	11,070	11,492	3.5	3.8
8	Australia	9,536	10,400	3.1	9.1
9	Costa Rica	9,233	8,322	2.5	-9.9
10	Japan	7,145	7,531	2.3	5.4
11	South Africa	5,782	6,042	1.8	4.5
12	Mexico	5,178	5,736	1.7	10.8
13	Czech Republic	4,610	4,777	1.4	3.6
14	India	4,181	4,704	1.4	12.5
15	Cuba	3,781	4,607	1.4	21.8
16	Denmark	4,632	4,457	1.3	-3.8
17	Greece	3,592	4,351	1.3	21.1
18	Ecuador	3,751	4,021	1.2	7.2
19	New Zealand	3,806	3,777	1.1	-0.8
20	South Korea	3,622	3,770	1.1	4.1
21	Peru	3,513	3,695	1.1	5.2
22	Netherlands	3,433	3,437	1.0	0.1
23	Argentina	3,846	3,422	1.0	-11.0
24	Austria	3,216	3,308	1.0	2.9
25	Chile	2,942	3,073	0.9	4.5
	WORLD TOTAL	**325,339**	**332,727**	**100.0**	**2.3**

HOST REGIONS*	2015/16 total	% of total	2016/17 total	% of total	% change
Europe	176,890	54.4	181,145	54.4	2.4
Latin America & Caribbean	53,105	16.3	51,513	15.5	-3.0
Asia	36,193	11.1	38,621	11.6	6.7
Oceania	13,815	4.2	14,639	4.4	6.0
Sub-Saharan Africa	12,738	3.9	13,433	4.0	5.5
Middle East & North Africa	6,844	1.9	6,901	2.1	14.2
North America	1,716	0.5	1,639	0.5	-4.5
Antarctica	87	0.0	46	0.0	-47.1
Multiple	24,751	7.6	24,790	7.5	0.2
TOTAL	**325,339**	**100.0**	**332,727**	**100.0**	

*Cyprus and Turkey are included in Europe. Mexico is included in Latin America.

OTHER FORMS OF EDUCATION ABROAD

In addition to the 332,727 U.S. students who received academic credit for study abroad in 2016/17, 414 institutions reported that an additional 38,975 U.S. students participated in non-credit work, internships, volunteering, and research abroad.

PARTICIPATION	US Study Abroad Total	US Higher Education Total	%
All U.S. undergrads studying abroad in academic year 2016/17	292,467	16,298,944*	1.8
All U.S. undergrads who study abroad during their degree program	292,467	2,692,398**	10.9
U.S. *Bachelor's students* who study abroad during their degree program	288,811	1,797,353***	16.0

*Total U.S. undergrad enrollment in the United States
**U.S. students receiving Associate and Bachelor's degrees
***U.S. students receiving Bachelor's degrees
Note: The numbers above do not include international students studying abroad.

DURATION	2015/16	2016/17
Short-term (summer, or eight weeks or less)	63.0	64.6
Mid-length (one semester, or one or two quarters)	34.6	33.1
Long-term (academic or calendar year)	2.4	2.3

2018 FACT SHEET:
MIDDLE EAST & NORTH AFRICA

REGIONAL TRENDS

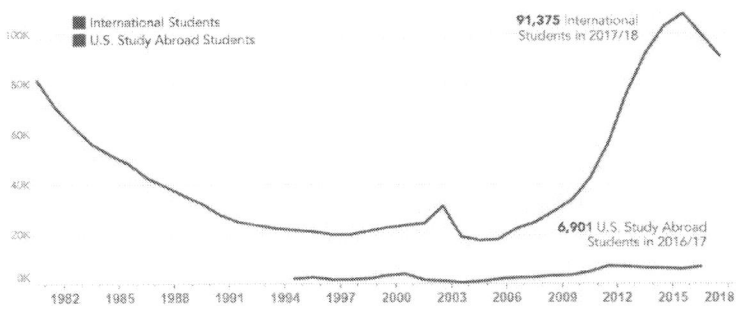

- International Students
- U.S. Study Abroad Students

91,375 International Students in 2017/18

6,901 U.S. Study Abroad Students in 2016/17

INTERNATIONAL STUDENTS BY PLACE OF ORIGIN

Place of Origin	2016/17	2017/18	% Change
Algeria	192	212	10.4
Bahrain	475	451	-5.1
Egypt	3,715	3,701	-0.4
Iran	12,643	12,783	1.1
Iraq	1,698	1,438	-15.3
Israel	2,393	2,327	-2.8
Jordan	2,312	2,420	4.7
Kuwait	9,825	10,190	3.7
Lebanon	1,556	1,633	4.9
Libya	1,311	1,064	-18.8
Morocco	1,634	1,563	-4.3
North Africa	7,544	7,268	-3.7
Oman	2,876	3,097	7.7
Palestinian Territories	423	480	13.5
Qatar	1,420	1,127	-20.6

Place of Origin	2016/17	2017/18	% Change
Saudi Arabia	52,611	44,432	-15.5
Syria	827	726	-12.2
Tunisia	692	728	5.2
United Arab Emirates	2,753	2,486	-9.7
Yemen	658	517	-21.4

INTERNATIONAL STUDENTS BY ACADEMIC LEVEL

Sub-Region	Undergraduate			Graduate			Non-degree			OPT		
	2016/17	2017/18	% Change	2016/17	2017/18	% Change	2016/17	2017/18	% Change	2016/17	2017/18	% Change
All Middle East & North Africa	53,151	48,543	-8.7	31,343	29,715	-5.2	9,219	6,591	-28.5	6,301	6,526	3.6
Middle East	50,009	45,534	-8.9	26,240	26,819	-5.0	8,760	6,173	-29.5	5,461	5,581	2.2
North Africa	3,142	3,009	-4.2	3,103	2,896	-6.7	459	418	-8.9	840	945	12.5

DESTINATIONS FOR U.S. STUDENTS STUDYING ABROAD

Destination	2015/16	2016/17	% Change	Destination	2015/16	2016/17	% Change
Algeria	0	1	-	Morocco	1,403	1,770	26.2
Bahrain	23	27	17.4	Oman	143	102	-28.7
Egypt	124	174	40.3	Palestinian Territories	15	17	13.3
Iran	3	1	-66.7	Qatar	122	108	-11.5
Iraq	1	2	100.0	Saudi Arabia	16	20	25.0
Israel	2,435	2,999	23.2	Syria	1	0	-100.0
Jordan	969	735	-24.1	Tunisia	19	11	-42.1
Kuwait	23	13	-43.5	United Arab Emirates	718	865	20.5
Lebanon	29	56	93.1	Yemen	0	0	0.0
Libya	0	0	0.0				

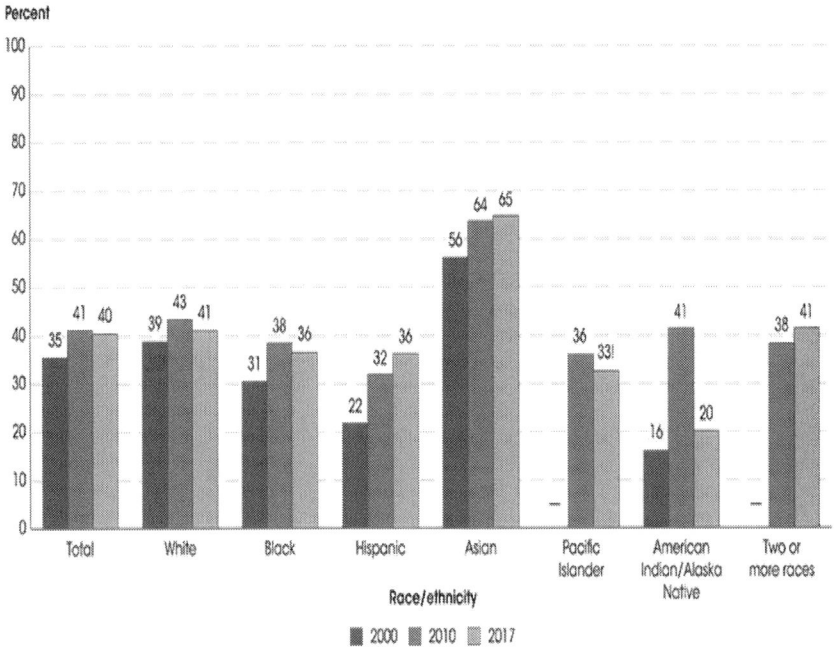

College enrollment rates of 18- to 24-year-olds, by race/ethnicity: 2000, 2010, and 2017

SOURCE: The Condition of Education 2019
National Center for Education Statistics (NCES)

Printed in Poland
by Amazon Fulfillment
Poland Sp. z o.o., Wrocław